WORLD OF CULTURE

CINEMA

by Kenneth W. Leish

Newsweek Books, New York

The Author and Editors make grateful acknowledgment for the use of quotations in the text from the following works:
Agee on Film, Volume I by James Agee © 1958 by the James Agee Trust. Reprinted by permission of Grosset & Dunlap, Inc.
Curtains by Kenneth Tynan. Copyright © 1952, 1961 by Kenneth Tynan. By permission of Atheneum Publishers, New York and Curtis Brown, Ltd.
"First Thoughts on *Potemkin*," by Wilton A. Barrett. Reprinted, with permission, from the *National Board of Review Magazine,* November, 1926.
Focus on D.W. Griffith, Harry M. Geduld, Editor, © 1971 by Harry M. Geduld. Reprinted by permission of Prentice-Hall, Inc.
Going Steady by Pauline Kael. Boston: Little Brown and Company.
Gotta Sing, Gotta Dance: Pictorial History of Film Musicals, by John Kobal. Reprinted by permission of the Hamlyn Publishing Group Ltd.
From Chapter 4, "Almost Purely Emotional," and Chapter 9, "A Succession of Masterpieces," *Movies: The History of Art and an Institution,* by Richard Schickel, © 1964 by Richard Schickel, published by Basic Books Inc., Publishers, New York.
Seventy Years of Cinema by Peter Cowie. Published by A.S. Barnes & Co. Inc.
The Fred Astaire and Ginger Rogers Book by Arlene Croce. Copyright © 1972 by Arlene Croce. Reprinted by permission of the publishers, Dutton—Sunrise, Inc., a subsidiary of E. P. Dutton & Co., Inc.
The Great Movies by William Bayer. A Ridge Press Book, published by Grosset & Dunlap, Inc.
The Great Movie Stars: The Golden Years by David Shipman. Reproduced by permission of the Hamlyn Publishing Group Ltd.
From *The History of World Cinema* by David Robinson. Copyright © 1973 by David Robinson. Reprinted with permission of Stein and Day Publishers and Methuen & Co., Ltd.
The Liveliest Art by Arthur Knight. Copyright © 1957 by Arthur Knight. Reprinted by permission of Macmillan Publishing Co., Inc.

Grateful acknowledgment is made for the use of excerpted material on pages 154–179 from the following works:
A Child of the Century by Ben Hecht. Copyright © 1954 by Ben Hecht. Reprinted by permission of Simon and Schuster.
Adventures with D.W. Griffith by Karl Brown, copyright © 1973 by Karl Brown. Reprinted with permission of Farrar, Straus & Giroux, Inc.
GWTW: The Making of Gone With the Wind by Gavin Lambert. Copyright © 1973 by Gavin Lambert. Reprinted by permission of Bantam Books.
From *Lillian Gish: The Movies, Mr. Griffith and Me* by Gish with Pinchot. Copyright © 1969 by Lillian Gish and Ann Pinchot. Published by Prentice-Hall, Inc. Englewood Cliffs, N.J.
To the Bodley Head for permission to include the extract from *My Autobiography* by Charles Chaplin.
By permission of G.P. Putnam's Sons from *On Cukor* by Gavin Lambert. Copyright © 1972 by Gavin Lambert.
From *Pentimento* by Lillian Hellman, copyright © 1973 by Lillian Hellman, by permission of Little, Brown and Co.
Run-through by John Houseman. Copyright © 1972 by John Houseman. Reprinted by permission of Simon and Schuster.
"And Did You Once See Irving Plain?" from *The Most of S.J. Perelman.* Copyright © 1957 by S.J. Perelman. Reprinted by permission of Simon and Schuster.
Reprinted with permission of Macmillan Publishing Co., Inc., from *The Name Above the Title* by Frank Capra. Copyright © 1971 by Frank Capra.
From *The Parade's Gone By . . . ,* by Kevin Brownlow. Copyright © 1968 by Kevin Brownlow. Reprinted by permission of Alfred A. Knopf, Inc.

ISBN: Regular edition 0-88225-109-0. ISBN: Deluxe edition 0-88225-110-4.
Library of Congress Catalog Card No. 73-89395
© 1974 Europa Verlag. All rights reserved. Printed and bound by Mondadori, Verona, Italy.

Contents

1

Opening Credits

THE VITASCOPE, A NEW PROCESS for the screen projection of movies, debuted triumphantly on April 23, 1896, at Koster and Bial's Music Hall in New York. It was, as the *Dramatic Mirror* told its readers a week later, a memorable evening:

> The first picture shown was the Leigh Sisters in their umbrella dance. The effect was the same as if the girls were there on the stage; all of their smiles and kicks and bows were seen. The second picture represented the breaking of waves on the seashore. Wave after wave came tumbling on the sand, and as they struck, broke into tiny floods just like the real thing. Some of the people in the front rows seemed to be afraid they were going to get wet, and looked about to see where they could run to, in case the waves came too close. . . . The Vitascope is a big success, and Mr. Edison is to be congratulated for his splendid contribution to the people's pleasure.

Since Thomas Edison had lent his name to the Vitascope venture, it was understandable that the *Dramatic Mirror* should offer him its congratulations and assume that the credit was his alone. In truth, however, the success of the Vitascope depended heavily on the work of another American inventor, Thomas Armat, and, although all devices for the screen projection of movies were based on breakthroughs made some years earlier in Edison's laboratories, the great man himself had little interest in motion pictures and no faith at all in their future.

Curiously enough, the inventor of the mimeograph, phonograph, and microphone took little interest in his colleagues' early experiments with a new and equally dramatic form of communication—the moving picture. As a result, credit for the development of the Edison Vitascope should properly be shared by a number of inventors, despite the fact that the name emblazoned across the credits opposite is that of the genius of Menlo Park.

The invention of the Vitascope represented the realization of an ancient dream, for man had been seeking a means of successfully simulating objects and creatures in motion for centuries. All sorts of optical entertainments, ranging from primitive shadow shows to elaborate panoramas and magic lantern presentations, had been developed in the seventeenth and eighteenth centuries. Then, in 1824, an English scientist named Peter Mark Roget discovered a principle that was to lead to a new wave of optical entertainments and eventually to moving pictures. The retina of the eye, Roget revealed, retains the impression of an object for a split second after that object has actually disappeared.

Throughout Europe imaginative men, fascinated by this principle of persistence of vision, worked on optical devices. On discs and drums and cylinders they drew pictures of objects in various stages of motion. When these devices were spun, the drawings—viewed through aper-

tures of one sort or another—appeared to be in continuous motion. Such primitive forms of animation could be viewed by only one person at a time, however, and the number of pictures that could be shown on a single disc was obviously quite limited.

The invention of photography in the 1830's opened new vistas to experimenters, and Thomas Edison was well aware of the many attempts made to capture motion with the camera. He knew, for instance, of the work of Eadweard Muybridge, whose remarkable series photographs were initially inspired by a question that had perplexed Governor Leland Stanford of California for years: When a horse runs, do all four of its feet ever leave the ground simultaneously? After several false starts—and a long interruption during which he was charged with the murder of his wife's lover—Muybridge was able to provide an affirmative answer to Stanford's question. Using as many as twenty-four cameras at a time, their shutters attached to wires strung across the racetrack and triggered by the galloping horse, he produced a fascinating series of pictures of horses in motion.

Another pioneer whom Edison knew personally was the Frenchman Etienne Jules Marey. Anxious to photograph birds in flight, Marey devised a "photographic rifle" that could take a dozen photographs in a single second on one revolving plate. Edison himself was far more interested in his phonograph than in photography, and he turned to the latter only when it seemed possible to him that pictures and sound might be produced on a single wax cylinder. Most of the research on this project was done by William K. L. Dickson, a brilliant young Englishman who had come to the United States in hopes of getting a job with Edison. The idea of combining pictures and sound proved impractical initially, and Edison soon lost interest in the venture. Dickson persevered, however, and when George Eastman marketed a thin, flexible roll film in 1889, the breakthrough became possible.

Edison, whose belated experiments with film (above) centered on attempts to link sound and motion, patented talking motion pictures in 1913. Others concentrated on motion itself—and in this area Eadweard Muybridge's series photographs of horses (top) are considered classics. No less important is the work of Etienne Marey (right below), a Frenchman whose "photographic rifle" produced the bird in flight at right above.

After devising a sprocket system for moving the film along, Dickson' completed the kinetograph camera. To show the exposed films, Dickson made the Kinetoscope, a four-foot-high peep show in which a battery-powered motor moved fifty-foot strips of film along a bank of spools; the film could be viewed through a magnifying lens as the images passed between an electric light and a revolving shutter. Edison's company patented both the Kinetoscope and kinetograph in the United States, but it was a measure of the inventor's lack of interest in the whole project that he refused to spend the $150 required to patent the equipment in Europe. It was a frugality that he regretted often in ensuing years.

Edison's staff began making films for the peep shows in 1893. A special tar-paper studio, affectionately called the Black Maria, was built in East Orange, New Jersey. It stood on a revolving platform and could be turned to take maximum advantage of the sunlight. There celebrities ranging from Annie Oakley and Buffalo Bill to boxer James Corbett and strongman Eugene Sandow cavorted for the camera, as did numerous dancing girls and trained animals. There, too, events as prosaic as a sneeze were immortalized on film. On April 14, 1894, the nation's first Kinetoscope parlor, licensed by Edison, was opened in New York. It was an overnight sensation, and people were soon lining up at penny arcades all over the country to deposit their coins, peer into machines, and see the brief films turned out in the Black Maria. The following year the Mutoscope, a similar peep show that was just different enough to avoid charges of patent infringement, opened and flourished. Among the most popular Mutoscope films was one entitled *Bridget Serves the Salad Undressed*, in which a maid misunderstands her instructions and, instead of leaving the dressing off the salad, serves it in her underwear.

Edison was content to reap the profits of his Kinetoscope venture, but throughout Europe and the United States those with greater vision devoted their lives to devising means of projecting movies on large

screens so that many people could enjoy them simultaneously. The early history of the cinema is marked by conflicting claims, and all that seems certain is that several men, working independently in different countries, developed or were on the verge of developing screen projectors at about the same time. Included among them were Robert W. Paul in England, the Lumière brothers in France, the brothers Max and Emil Skladanowsky in Germany, and Thomas Armat, C. Francis Jenkins, and the Lathams—a father and two sons—in the United States. All deserve a place in the history of the movies, but who did what exactly when is difficult, if not impossible, to determine.

When Edison realized how close others were coming to perfecting screen projectors he began to develop his own equipment. He promptly encountered difficulties, however, and decided instead to accept an offer made to him on behalf of Thomas Armat, who had perfected the stop-motion device that was essential to screen projection. Edison manufactured the machine for Armat and lent his name and prestige to what became known as the Vitascope.

Edison's efforts came too late, however, and consequently it is the Lumières who are usually credited with the first public projection of movies on a large screen. Louis Jean Lumière and his elder brother Auguste Marie were the sons of a photographer who also manufactured photographic equipment. It was natural, therefore, for them to be fascinated by Edison's Kinetoscope, and it was fitting that they were the ones, in February, 1895, to invent a single machine that could both photograph and project movies. Only thirty people came to the first public exhibition of the Lumières' Cinématographe, which was held in Paris on December 28, 1895, in the Salon Indien, the basement lounge of the Grand Café. Within a short time, however, the show was the rage of Paris; everyone wanted to see such startling films as *The*

The enterprising Lumière brothers, Louis Jean and Auguste Marie, were the first to project movies onto a large screen. The Sprinkler Sprinkled (right), one of their popular short films, was featured in advertising (below) for their Cinématographe.

Arrival of the Mail Train and *The Sprinkler Sprinkled.* (In the latter, a young boy squeezes a gardener's hose, the gardener looks into the nozzle to see why the water has stopped, the boy releases the hose, the gardener gets a faceful of water, and the boy gets a well-deserved spanking.) The Lumières exhibited with equal success in other European capitals, and by 1897 their catalogue of available films listed no fewer than 358 items, including such gems as *The Unveiling of a Monument to William I, Parts I, II, and III.*

The Lumières' Cinématographe opened in New York in July, 1896, three months after the debut of the Vitascope. Audiences flocked to Keith's Union Square Theater to see *The Charge of the Seventh French Cuirassiers, The Arrival of the Mail Train,* and *Baby's Breakfast.* The *Dramatic Mirror* thought the Cinématographe superior to the Vitascope and other processes: ". . . the pictures are clearer and there is less vibration, so that the pictures are not so trying to the eye as those produced by other machines."

Late that year still another process, the American Biograph, made its debut. Using considerably larger film than the Vitascope and the Cinématographe and projecting twice as many pictures per minute as its rivals, the Biograph, which was partly the work of Edison's former colleague William Dickson, threw the largest, brightest, and steadiest picture of all. Among the most popular Biograph films was one taken by a camera mounted on the front of a moving train in Conway, North Wales, and one in which the famous actor Joseph Jefferson performed excerpts from his hit play about Rip Van Winkle. Other Biograph favorites showed Presidential candidate William McKinley on his front porch in Canton, Ohio, and the speeding Empire State Express, which made Lumière's mail train film seem tame.

The simple fact that Lumière equipment was easily transported gave that company an edge over its competitors in Europe. All across the Continent itinerant showmen could be found, moving from fairground

to fairground and exhibiting films to enthusiastic audiences—some of whom had the great pleasure of seeing themselves in crowd scenes photographed earlier in the day. In the United States, however, the novelty of the movies soon wore thin. Authentic and spurious films of the Spanish-American War attracted large audiences, and an Edison film entitled *The Kiss,* in which stage performers May Irwin and mustachioed John C. Rice recreated an embrace they were enacting nightly on Broadway, titillated some viewers while offending others. For the most part, however, the films being shown lacked any semblance of creativity or imagination. Having seen one film of parading soldiers or speeding trains, audiences found it easy to eschew others of the same sort. As a result, vaudeville house managers came to regard films as "chasers," placed last on the bill to help empty the house.

One vaudeville theater in Rochester, New York, tried a rather unusual method to boost ticket sales. "There will be plenty of fun at Wonderland next week," promised the Rochester *Post-Express* in 1897. "In one of the cinematographic views to be shown the machine will be run backward. The scene selected for this curious experiment is the one representing the crossing of the Saône River by the mounted French dragoons. After the troopers reach the other side of the stream the picture machine will be reversed and the men and horses will immediately start backward across the river, the scene closing with the horses backing up the steep bank down which they had plunged but a few moments before. Whatever else it may prove the experiment will at least be a curious novelty and one which everyone who has seen the Cinématographe will be desirous to witness. . . ."

Fortunately for the future of the movies, two genuinely creative men—George Méliès in France and Edwin S. Porter in the United States—were about to demonstrate that films could do far more than

merely record everyday life. Méliès, a professional magician and theater operator who had seen the Lumière show at the Salon Indien, thought that the new device could be used effectively in his magic act. After buying a camera in England and building his own projector, he began photographing everything in sight. One day while Méliès was recording a truck moving down the street, his camera jammed; by the time filming resumed, a hearse occupied the spot on which the truck had stood. When Méliès viewed the finished film later, he saw a truck turn miraculously into a hearse. Film, he realized, could be manipulated in countless ways, and scenes could be staged for the camera. In time Méliès developed such new techniques as the fade-out, overlap dissolve, double exposure, fast and slow motion, and animation.

In a specially built studio, Méliès turned out more than a thousand films between 1896 and 1914. They ranged from brief shorts—among them one in which an actor's clothes keep returning to his body as he strives desperately to get undressed and another in which an actor takes off his head and places it on a table—to much longer films, some of which ran for twenty minutes. This latter group included *Cinderella*, *An Impossible Voyage*, and his most famous film, *A Trip to the*

Moon, which was made in 1902 and which featured a large, elaborately costumed cast, lavish sets, animation, and a grab bag of visual tricks. The story, such as it was, concerned a group of astronomers traveling to the moon. From the catalogue of an American company that illegally duplicated the film and sold it under the title *A Trip to Mars* comes this synopsis of a memorable sequence:

> In the midst of the clouds the moon is visible at a distance. The shell [spaceship] coming closer every minute, the moon magnifies rapidly until finally it attains colossal dimensions. It gradually assumes the shape of a living, grotesque face, smiling sanctimoniously. Suddenly the shell arrives with the rapidity of lightning, and pierces the eye of the moon. The face at once makes horrible grimaces, whilst enormous tears flow from the wound.

Taken prisoner by the strange inhabitants of the moon, the astronomers escape when they realize that their captors are so fragile that they burst into a thousand pieces when struck.

Enormously popular in their day, the films of Méliès were shown, often without his permission, all over the United States and Europe. Today some critics find them tedious, but in their day they were regarded as charming and witty, and Méliès's position as the first artist of the cinema is indisputable. "I owe him everything," D.W. Griffith was to say when his own career was at its zenith.

Edwin S. Porter, who was in charge of the Edison Company studios and acted as scriptwriter, cameraman, and director for most of the films made there, was also enormously impressed by the films of Méliès, which he studied carefully. Agreeing with the French pioneer that films should tell stories, he rummaged through the Edison Company archives and found several films showing various companies of firemen and fire-fighting equipment in action. Using excerpts from these films, supplemented by freshly-shot footage, he spliced together a new film, *The Life of an American Fireman*. Beginning with a firehouse scene, the film shows a man dreaming of his wife and child, who appear in a dream balloon. Then, in the first close-up in an American movie, a hand is seen pulling a fire alarm. The firehouse springs to life as the men dress, slide down poles, race to their equipment, and speed off to the fire. Inside a burning house, a woman and child are in danger. The woman is saved first, and a brave fireman goes back for the child. Here at last were characters with whom audiences could identify. And Por-

In 1898 American Biograph sent armed cameramen (above) into battle—to capture the Spanish-American War on film. The equipment these men used was only slightly more sophisticated than that developed by the Lumières (right), but film-making itself was steadily improving. By 1910, for instance, cutting, splicing, and editing had become routine practice in most film studios (left above).

ter's cutting from scenes of the firemen to scenes of the trapped victims added an urgency and excitement that was new to films.

Since Porter had taken segments from different films, several different fire companies were shown in *The Life of an American Fireman*, which purported to be about just one unit. Unabashed, the Edison Company capitalized on that weakness, stating that they "were compelled to enlist the services of the fire departments of four different cities. It will be difficult for the exhibitor to conceive the . . . number of rehearsals necessary to turn out a film of this kind."

The entertainment value of the moving picture was appreciated from the first by such giants of the early cinema as George Méliès and Edwin S. Porter. The former, a Frenchman, was the first to experiment with animation, most spectacularly in a 1902 short called A Trip to the Moon *(opposite). Porter, the director of Edison's studios, was responsible for* The Great Train Robbery, *an immensely popular film that featured an irrelevant but startling close-up, seen at right, of an outlaw firing directly at the camera. No sequence in the short history of the cinema had so directly involved the audience in the action—and the infatuation born in that moment was to endure for decades to come.*

Later in that same year, 1903, Porter made *The Great Train Robbery*, which was destined to become the most popular film of the decade. Lasting less than twelve minutes, it told the simple but exciting story of a gang of desperadoes who hold up a mail train, terrorize a small western town, and are chased and finally killed by a posse. Here was the precursor of all the Westerns, chase scenes, and cops and robbers films that were to become staples of the movie industry. But *The Great Train Robbery* was important for other reasons as well. Porter crosscut between events that were happening simultaneously, instead of slavishly telling his story in chronological order. When, for instance, he cut from a shot of the fleeing bandits to one of a young girl finding the telegraph operator bound and gagged, he was indicating that the two sequences were happening at the same time. This device, called "parallel editing," was a notable advance in narrative technique. Also noteworthy was the relative freedom with which the camera was moved to follow the actors in the many outdoor scenes.

Filmed as part of *The Great Train Robbery* was a scene that the Edison catalogue described thus: "Scene 14.—REALISM. A life size picture of Barnes, leader of the outlaw band, taking aim and firing point blank at each individual in the audience. (This effect is gained by foreshortening in making the picture.) The resulting excitement is great. This section of the scene can be used either to begin the subject or end it, as the operator may choose."

The scene had nothing to do with the plot of the movie, but audiences didn't care. They loved the close-up and they loved *The Great Train Robbery*, and thereafter they would go to the nickelodeons and "Electric Theaters" that were beginning to open everywhere, not to see films that only mirrored reality but to enjoy movies that would engross, excite, and thrill them with stories of romance and adventure.

17

2

Window to a Wider World

"HERE ARE THE INGREDIENTS of a 5-cent theater," reported *The Moving Picture World and View Photographer* in its issue of May 4, 1907: "One storeroom, seating from 200 to 500 persons. One phonograph with extra large horn. One young woman cashier. One electric sign. One cinematograph, with operator. One canvas on which to throw the pictures. One piano. One barker. One manager. As many chairs as the store will hold. A few brains and a little tact. Mix pepper and salt to taste. After that all you have to do is open the doors, start the phonograph and carry the money to the bank. The public does the rest."

Movies may have been chasers in the vaudeville houses that catered to the middle and upper classes, but to the poor they were a fabulous window to a wider world; they offered escape, entertainment, and instruction. Between 1905 and 1908 at least ten thousand nickelodeons opened in the United States alone; thousands more prospered in Europe. In abandoned storefronts, unused lecture halls, and former penny arcades, these shabby pleasure palaces offered movies from morning till midnight.

To be sure, some of the nickelodeons were fancier than others, and some of these "Bijou Dreams" and "Electric Theaters" did cater to the middle class. They offered live songs between films, and they flashed advertisements and advice—"Ladies, Kindly Remove Your Hats"—on the screen. Some provided elaborate sound effects, too, as *The Moving Picture World* discussed in a 1907 issue:

If any single figure can fairly be said to symbolize the glory years of the silent film—the cinema's truly international epoch—it is Charles Chaplin's indomitable tramp. The Little Fellow, as millions came to call him, was at once tatty and debonair, browbeaten and irrepressibly optimistic—and he was, without question, the best-loved international star in all of film history.

. . . the sound of horses' hooves upon a paved street is made very realistic by the use of a pair of cocoanut shells which are applied to a marble slab in a corresponding manner to the gait of a horse. . . . Sand paper blocks are another useful article and have a number of uses, the escape of steam from a locomotive, exhaust from an automobile, splash of water and a number of other effects are produced by this common article. A dozen whistles, bells, pieces of steel and broken glass are also brought into use.

Because nickelodeons often changed their bills daily, there was an insatiable market for new films, and film-makers on both sides of the Atlantic sought rewarding careers in the new medium. Since films were silent, language was no barrier—titles could easily be translated—and the result was a truly international era of film-making. During the first decade of the twentieth century, France dominated the international film industry. Charles Pathé, in particular, quickly built himself a motion picture empire that controlled the manufacture of projectors and film, made and distributed movies, and owned theaters as well. His director of production was Ferdinand Zecca, who became famous for the "chase" films that were wildly popular wherever movies were shown. In each, some normal occurrence precipitated a fantastic chase in which acrobatics, trick photography of all kinds, and remarkable cinematic inventiveness combined to create a lunatic, almost surrealistic world. Pathé's biggest star during those years was Max Linder. The gifted comedian always portrayed an elegantly dressed gentleman who got himself in any number of embarrassing predicaments but emerged unscathed due to his own resourcefulness. Linder made more than four hundred films between 1905 and 1914 and, along with Danish actress Asta Nielsen, ranks as one of the first international film stars.

Pathé and his colleagues found a new trove in 1908 when they began presenting so-called "films d'art" in which the world's greatest stage stars appeared in classic roles. Sarah Bernhardt, Réjane, and others of similar stature played in pretentious films that nevertheless lent a new respectability to motion pictures.

If the French dominated the movie industry in those early years, the Italians nevertheless carved out for themselves a lucrative piece of the market. Italian costume spectacles were famous around the world for their enormous casts and lavish sets, and the most famous of all was *Quo Vadis*, a 1912 film that took two hours to unreel and had enough Christians, lions, and extras for a dozen films. In the United States short films were to remain the rule for some time, due in large part to the reluctance of the leading production companies to tamper with an already prosperous business. During the early 1900's dozens of independent film-makers were cranking out "quickies"—melodramas, .comedies, cheap versions of classic novels, and recreations of such current events as the Sanford White murder—that found a ready market in the rapidly multiplying nickelodeons. Most of these films were marked by static camera work, inadequate lighting, unconvincing sets, and acting that was, to say the least, rudimentary. Professional actors worked in films only when stage roles were unavailable; often they were expected to do odd jobs around the set when they were not actually filming.

As the movie business became increasingly profitable, Edison grew more and more resentful of the numerous rivals who were capitalizing on what he regarded as his invention. Recognizing that he could not fight all his competitors, he invited the major companies—Vitagraph, Biograph, Kalem, Lubin, Selig, Essanay, Kleine, and the French firms Méliès and Pathé—to join him in forming the Motion Picture Patents Company. In 1909 the consortium announced that henceforth no one else could legally photograph or print movies in the United States or in the major European countries. The group then founded the General Film Company to extend their monopoly to film distribution. All exhibitors were told that they would have to pay a two-dollar weekly licensing fee for the privilege of showing films made by members of the Patents Company.

By 1910 the fledgling film industry had already produced a handful of recognized stars, among them Danish actress Asta Nielsen (above). The best known of these headliners was French comedian Max Linder (top), who starred in some four hundred films for the first movie mogul, Charles Pathé. Short features remained the staple fare in American movie houses, but Europe was developing a taste for costume spectaculars. Foremost among these was Quo Vadis *(right), an Italian film of 1912.*

For Edison, it was a case of too little too late. The movie business had attracted a number of clever, ambitious men, many of them European immigrants, who had no intention of being shut out of the growing industry. Carl Laemmle, Adolph Zukor, William Fox, and others fought the Patents Company openly or surreptitiously, and with the aid of exhibitors who deeply resented the company's tactics they succeeded in circumventing the legal snares set by Edison and his colleagues. Independent films flourished as never before, and eventually the monopoly was declared officially dead in the courts.

The battle against the Patents Company had several unforeseen results. Among them was the establishment of Hollywood as a center of film production, a result of the independent producers' discovery that the company was far less likely to harass them if they operated on the West Coast rather than in New York. The Los Angeles suburb also offered perpetual sunshine and cheap labor, and it was conveniently close to Mexico in case the Patents Company turned the police against them. By 1915 more than half of all American movies were being made in Hollywood.

Another important new development was the star system. Film company executives had long realized that anonymous players would accept low salaries, whereas famous ones would demand large sums of money. Thus, while audiences clamored for information about "the Biograph Girl" and other favorite performers, producers steadfastly refused to reveal their names. Carl Laemmle, the most aggressive of the independents, broke down the barriers when he wooed Florence Lawrence, the most popular Biograph leading lady, away to his own company in 1910. Laemmle then planted the story that Lawrence had been killed in a streetcar accident in St. Louis. Subsequently, he heatedly denied the rumor, accused Biograph of having invented the dastardly story in hopes of ending Lawrence's career, and arranged for the actress to vist St. Louis in person. When she did, she was mobbed by hysterical fans who tore off pieces of her clothing as souvenirs. The star system, with all its glory and all its excesses, had arrived.

At the height of this chaotic era the man who was to transform the movies into an art form arrived on the scene. David Wark Griffith, scion of a Southern family that had seen better days, was thirty-three when he tried to sell some scenarios to the Edison Company in 1907. His stories were rejected, but he was hired as an actor. Accepting the job only because he needed the money—twenty dollars for four days' work in an epic called *Rescued from an Eagle's Nest*—Griffith began a movie career that was to span more than twenty years. In 1908 he went to work for Biograph, where he was given his first directorial assignment. Within the next five years he turned out no fewer than five hundred short films. Working with cameraman Billy Bitzer, an artist in his own right, Griffith created movies that critics and audiences alike recognized as unique. The quality varied, of course; a consistently high level of achievement was virtually impossible for Griffith and Bitzer, who were cranking out two or three films a week. But almost every one of the films contained some new experiment in screen technique, some new stretching of the medium's capabilities. Biograph's business soared as audiences eagerly awaited the Griffith films.

The tendency today is to credit Griffith with having invented everything. The reputable *Columbia Encyclopedia*, for instance, says that Griffith "introduced the fade-in, the fade-out, the long shot, the full shot, the close-up, the moving camera shot, the flashback, crosscut-

To escape the monopolistic stranglehold of the Patents Company, independent film-makers migrated westward after 1909. Relocating in Hollywood, California (above), a bucolic community beyond the reach of Edison's lawyers, these pioneering producers laid the foundations of a vast new commercial empire. By 1915, more than half of all American movies were being made in Hollywood, which had become a bustling metropolis (right above).

ting, and juxtaposition. He initiated rehearsals before shooting a scene and took great pains with lighting effects." Actually, many of the innovations credited to Griffith had been used before by film-makers. What Griffith did was to define and refine them all, creating a total screen technique. Instead of having a static camera shoot a scene from one spot, he filmed each scene from many angles and pieced the sequence together in the editing room in a manner that heightened and controlled the dramatic impact. Harry M. Geduld, a Griffith scholar, put it this way: "Griffith's advances over Porter—to whom the movie camera was seldom more than an objective or impartial recorder of the dramatic scene—were essentially 1) to turn the movie camera into an *active* observer, and 2) to demonstrate how, in filming any story, it was the inherent *dramatic ideas* that had to determine the selection, sequence, and timing of the shots (or 'incomplete actions') that were filmed, and then assembled in the process of editing. From Griffith's method of editing through 'dramatic continuity' all motion picture techniques have been evolved."

Griffith's desire to make longer films was thwarted by Biograph. But in 1912 Adolph Zukor released in the United States a four-reel French film starring Sarah Bernhardt as Queen Elizabeth. The profits were enormous, but they were overshadowed the next year when the Italian spectacle *Quo Vadis* finally opened on Broadway in a legitimate theater. Audiences cheerfully paid a dollar and a half apiece to see the full-length feature. The Patents Company fumed, but it was obvious that longer films were what the customers wanted.

Determined to make the greatest movie ever produced, Griffith left Biograph in 1913 and soon set to work on a film version of Thomas Dixon's novel of the Civil War, *The Clansman*. The result of his labors was *The Birth of a Nation*, which exploded on the screen in 1915. Filmed at a cost of one hundred thousand dollars, the three-hour epic was enormously popular and equally controversial; it is still regarded as one of the key films in cinema history.

The Birth of a Nation combines documentary reenactments of historical moments—such as Sherman's march to the sea and Lincoln's assassination—with the fictitious story of two families' experiences during the war and the subsequent period of Reconstruction. The Southern family, the Camerons, are ideally happy; parents and children

are kind and loving and even their slaves are content. The Stoneman children of Pennsylvania are friends of the Camerons—several potential romances are hinted at among the sons and daughters—but their father is a fanatical abolitionist. The war inflicts suffering on both families, but after the fighting ends the woes of the Camerons and their Southern neighbors increase. Incited by Stoneman and other Northerners, the freed slaves humiliate their former masters, rape the white women —one of the Cameron girls leaps to her death from a cliff to avoid violation—and seize political control. It is the newly-formed Ku Klux Klan that saves the day, its hooded heroes thundering to the rescue of the Camerons, who have been besieged by blacks and scalawags. The Klan takes control, subjugates the rebels, and saves the South from humiliation and anarchy.

The film's depiction of leering, bestial blacks created a furor throughout the country, and much to Griffith's surprise and dismay the movie was roundly condemned by many fair-minded Americans. But although Griffith's view of history and race relations was deplorable, his artistry was undeniable. It was, as critic Bosley Crowther has written, "as though a superb symphony had burst from the muck of primitive music within two decades after the invention of the horn. . . . People were simply bowled over by its vivid pictorial sweep, its arrangements of personal involvements, its plunging of the viewer into a sea of boiling historical associations. . . ."

Any follow-up to *The Birth of a Nation* should have been anticlimactic, but Griffith's next film, *Intolerance*, was even more monu-

mental. The two-million-dollar film told not one story but four. Ancient Babylon, Biblical Judea, sixteenth-century France, and modern America were the scenes of its four tales of bigotry and intolerance, and Griffith cut back and forth from one story to another with increasing rapidity as the film progressed. By the last reel, the crosscutting was almost frantic. Scenes of a girl rushing to warn the Babylonian king that he has been betrayed were intercut with sequences showing the lover of the French heroine running through the streets to save her from the anti-Huguenots, Christ carrying his cross to Calvary, and the modern heroine racing to obtain a pardon that will stay her husband's execution. Despite Griffith's ability to focus on intimate scenes in the midst of staggering spectacle, and despite his brilliant use of crosscutting to heighten tension and involvement, *Intolerance* was a commercial failure. Audiences found it confusing and unappealing. Griffith was both heartbroken and financially ruined.

In 1915 Griffith had founded the Triangle Film Corporation, a partnership involving two other men who rank high among the innovators of early Hollywood. The first was Mack Sennett, a former actor who had studied Griffith's work at Biograph and had, by 1912, talked two former bookies to whom he was in debt into financing Keystone, his California studio. Sennett did not direct the Keystone comedies himself, but he did supervise every step of preliminary planning and postproduction editing from his suite atop a tower overlooking the studio. Nothing was sacred in the Sennett comedies, and a marvelously talented group of performers—including cross-eyed Ben Turpin, rotund Fatty Arbuckle, lovely Mabel Normand, and, for a time, Charlie Chaplin himself—mocked the formal and the pretentious while engaging in outrageous slapstick.

The highlight of the Keystone comedies was always a hilarious chase, sometimes involving Sennett's famous bathing beauties but always featuring the memorable Keystone Kops. "If there is one symbol of the art of Sennett," film historian Richard Schickel writes, "it is of the Kops, mounted on a decrepit flivver, their blue-clad arms and legs protruding in wild tangles, their faces set in masks of stolid dignity, pursuing a miscreant through the wastelands of Southern California. . . . A wild swerve around a trolley car, a near miss of a wandering mongrel, a brush of a bumper with a speeding train, the sudden disembarkation as the car crashes against tree or hydrant (how was it that the Kops always missed the moving targets and hit the stationary ones?). Then the chase on foot, through the alleys and backyards, in which all the sprinklers were unaccountably turned on, finally the quarry coming to ground, naturally, in a pastry shop or restaurant offering its tempting array of missiles to be hurled by one and all."

The third partner at Triangle was Thomas Ince, whose name means little to today's filmgoers but whom historians regard as the prototype of the creative producer. Like Sennett, Ince began as an actor and director at Biograph, founded his own studio, and began carefully supervising productions rather than directing them himself. After a scenario had been approved for filming, Ince stamped "produce as written" on it, and any Ince employee who forgot that stricture lived to

regret it. Ince dramas and Westerns were marked by straightforward stories, tight construction, believable characters, and lots of clear, fast action. He knew what audiences liked and gave it to them, raising the artistic level of the movies at the same time. "Ince had a great influence on films," director John Ford said, "for he tried to make them move."

One of Ince's most important stars was William S. Hart, the first great Western hero. He had been preceded as a cowboy star by "Broncho Billy" Anderson, an Easterner who had no experience with horses. (Given a bit part in *The Great Train Robbery*, he had actually fallen off his horse during shooting.) Anderson recognized a moneymaking opportunity when he saw one, however, and under the aegis of his own Essanay Studios he appeared in a lucrative series of Westerns between 1908 and 1915. These first Westerns bore little relationship to the real West, and the portly Anderson could not have been a more unlikely cowboy. William S. Hart, on the other hand, was an authentic Westerner who had grown up among trail hands and Indians and who spoke fluent Sioux by the time he was six. He subsequently became a successful Shakespearean actor in New York, but when films became a respectable occupation he asked Thomas Ince for a chance to portray

the West realistically on the screen. In his films Hart played the good bad man, the hero who followed his own moral code and was redeemed of his sins by the love of a good woman. There was a sense of poetry as well as realism in Hart's films, and the characters he played had great dignity. The very titles of his movies—*The Cradle of Courage*, *The Testing Block*—indicate the degree to which Hart's West was a man's world where strength and purpose were requisites of survival.

The other major star who flourished under Ince's guidance was Douglas Fairbanks, who portrayed the brash, capable, all-American boy in a series of farces that ridiculed the pretensions of modern life. A happy-go-lucky optimist, the Fairbanks character was a city dweller but one who had the physical strength to surmount any crisis that might arise. "Douglas Fairbanks is a tonic," a French critic wrote. "He smiles and you feel relieved." When Fairbanks married Mary Pickford in 1920, they were indisputably Hollywood's royal couple.

No star has ever been more adored than Pickford. Although her appeal may elude today's filmgoers, she was in her time the most popular woman in the world and probably the best paid. Hired by Biograph in 1909, the year she turned sixteen, "Little Mary" quickly won the affection of a wide audience who loved her curls and coyness. She was earning one thousand dollars a week by 1914, and ten times that much soon thereafter. On screen she played the plucky virgin, her optimism made palatable by a basic awareness of reality. Even when she was in her mid-twenties, her fans insisted that she portray such characters as *A Poor Little Rich Girl* and *Rebecca of Sunnybrook Farm*. Although she would have preferred to graduate to more sophisticated roles, she was pleased by her salary, which by 1917 had escalated to more than a million dollars a year.

At the opposite end of the purity scale was Theda Bara, née Theodosia Goodman of Cincinnati, Ohio, but passed off to fans as the love child of a European adventurer and an Arab princess. Her screen name itself was an anagram of Arab death, and she was said to have been weaned on serpent's blood. This most *fatale* of all *femmes* was often photographed by her employers, Fox Studios, in the company of various skulls and skeletons, which were said to be the remains of men who had loved her. Her first film, a 1915 vehicle entitled *A Fool There Was*, allowed Bara to glare and arch her back while otherwise sensible men ruined their lives for love of her. In films such as *Salome* and *Cleopatra* she was to play the vampire supreme, and for a few years she enjoyed extraordinary popularity. Then, inexplicably, audiences began to laugh rather than sigh at such vamping, and Bara made a reluctant exit. She had made a fortune for Fox and for herself, however, and she had proved that with the right ingredients the Hollywood publicity mills could create a star, at least temporarily.

Among the other popular stars of the era were the matinee idols J. Warren Kerrigan, King Baggott, and Francis X. Bushman, whose marriage to costar Beverly Bayne was kept secret by Metro lest Bushman's fans desert him. Clara Kimball Young, Alice Joyce, Pauline Frederick, and Marguerite Clark all had fervent fans, and moviegoers eagerly awaited the serial adventures of Pearl White, a pretty blond whose

In 1915, the year Intolerance *was released, Griffith formed the Triangle Film Company. His first partner in the new venture was a former actor named Mack Sennett (in shirt-sleeves at left above), who was to bring his distinctive touch to hundreds of slapstick comedies. These short films varied only in their particulars—for each featured a protracted chase scene involving the Keystone Kops (left), and each included a number of Sennett's bathing beauties (above).*

past experience as a trapeze performer stood her in good stead when she did her own stunts for *The Perils of Pauline*. Attacked by Indians, thrown off cliffs, tied to railroad tracks, and dangled over carnivorous beasts, Pearl always survived to appear in the next episode.

Of all the early stars, however, none is more esteemed today than Charles Chaplin, one of the cinema's few authentic geniuses. No names were required on marquees when a Chaplin picture was playing; a photograph of Charlie in his tramp costume was enough to pack theaters all over the world. Chaplin came to show business after an impoverished childhood in England, and vaudeville was his escape route from the slums. While touring in the United States with the Karno Comedy Company, he was spotted by Mack Sennett and eventually signed to a Keystone contract at one hundred and fifty dollars a week. Chaplin made thirty-five films for Sennett in 1914, many of which he was permitted to direct himself. Early in that year he devised the tramp costume that was to become internationally famous. Improvising from the Keystone wardrobe department and from the belongings of other play-

ers, he combined baggy pants, a tight jacket, a derby, oversized shoes, a cane, and—as a touching sign of human vanity—a small mustache. The Little Fellow, as the tramp would be known, did not fully emerge at Keystone, however; the pace of film-making there was too frantic to permit Chaplin's inventiveness to flower fully. But his Keystone comedies, especially the delightful *Tillie's Punctured Romance*, made him a star, and when he left Sennett at the end of 1914 it was to accept a far more generous offer from Essanay. In the next four years, Chaplin made thirty more one-reel, two-reel, and three-reel comedies in which

his unique artistry was at last revealed. Happily, his popularity also grew, and by 1917 he was able to command a million dollars for making eight films over an eighteen-month period.

"Of all comedians," James Agee has written of Chaplin, "he worked most deeply and most shrewdly within a realization of what a human being is, and is up against. The Tramp is as centrally representative of humanity, as many-sided and as mysterious as Hamlet, and it seems unlikely that any dancer or actor can have excelled him in eloquence, variety, and poignancy of motion." Chaplin's Little Fellow had a resilience and optimism that neither cruelty nor ridicule could extinguish; it was his indomitable spirit that made audiences love him.

By the end of World War I, American films had achieved a worldwide dominance they would maintain for more than a quarter of a century. European production had been all but halted by the war, and moviegoers of all nations had adopted Chaplin, Fairbanks, Hart, and the other American stars as their own. The elegant new movie palaces that were opening in cities all over the world showed films made in the United States. And everywhere the name of "Hollywood" had become a synonym for "movies."

3

The International Epoch

SURPRISINGLY, IT WAS IN DEFEATED GERMANY that European film-making enjoyed its postwar renaissance. There, chiefly at the subsidized UFA studios (Universam-Film-Aktiengesellschaft), an extraordinarily talented group of directors, writers, and cameramen created an exciting series of movies that for several years made Germany the artistic center of the cinema.

The first German films to win international popularity were compelling costume dramas that took considerable liberty with historical facts but nevertheless presented convincing portraits of famous personages. The artful, ironic touch of director Ernst Lubitsch was evident in *Anne Boleyn, Madame DuBarry*, and others of the genre, movies that were advertised as "European" or "Scandinavian" films abroad lest anti-German sentiment keep audiences away. Retitled *Passion* in the United States, *Madame DuBarry* attracted 106,000 people to one Broadway theater in a single week and thereby put Lubitsch and the film's star, Polish actress Pola Negri, high on the list of Continental talent coveted by Hollywood.

The Cabinet of Dr. Caligari, made in 1919, was not especially successful at the box office, but it was nonetheless a unique film and one that has found a secure place in film history. The movie is narrated by a young man who suspects Dr. Caligari, a mountebank appearing with a traveling fair, of being responsible for a series of violent crimes. It is soon revealed that Caligari's instrument of death is Cesare, a cadaverlike somnambulist who is completely controlled by the evil doctor. The heroine, Jane, is abducted by Cesare at Caligari's order. She escapes, and in the subsequent search for the doctor it is discovered that he is really the director of a local insane asylum, in which the narrator is an unwilling inmate.

Some fifty-five years after its premiere screening, The Cabinet of Dr. Caligari *remains the supreme example of expressionistic film-making. Macabre sets, surreal lighting effects, and distorted props (opposite) all consciously evoke the highly theatrical, singularly menacing world of expressionistic art, which was enjoying a vogue in postwar Germany at the time Robert Wiene's film was made.*

Directed by Robert Wiene from a script by Carl Mayer and Hans Janowitz, *Caligari* uses expressionistic sets and lighting to reflect the narrator's madness. Walls are trapezoidal, windows triangular; weird effects of light and shadow are painted directly on the sets; props are oversized, and both makeup and acting are deliberately macabre. The evocation of a nightmare world of insanity is complete.

Caligari was one of a kind, however. More influential were the so-called "street films" that dealt realistically and sympathetically with the lives of common men. Most notable was F. W. Murnau's *The Last*

33

Laugh, distinguished by that director's pictorial inventiveness and by his strikingly effective use of a mobile camera. Written by Carl Mayer and photographed by Karl Freund, two of the most brilliant German film-makers, *The Last Laugh* stars Emil Jannings as a proud and respected hotel doorman who is suddenly demoted to the humiliating post of lavatory attendant. Under Murnau's direction, the camera follows Jannings, exploring his world and his relationships and underlining his emotions. When, for instance, Jannings steals the doorman's uniform, which means so much to him, he looks back guiltily at the hotel, which seems to sway menacingly. When he gets drunk, the camera whirls dizzily. Murnau and his colleagues were able to bring the doorman and his plight to life so completely that no subtitles were required to explain what was happening, an unusual omission at the time.

The camera work in *Variety*, directed in 1925 by E. A. Dupont with Freund again behind the camera, was even more dazzling. The story—about a trapeze artist who kills his wife's lover—provided an opportunity for the camera to swing through the air with the trapeze artists and to plunge to earth when one of them falls to his death. That same year also marked the release of G. W. Pabst's *The Joyless Street*, an uncompromisingly realistic story of inflation-plagued Vienna that was remarkable for its innovative camera angles. "The butcher, always with a huge white hound by his side, is invariably photographed from below," critic Arthur Knight points out, "suggesting his domination over the people of the street. The professor in his bare apartment (much of his furniture has been pawned for food) is generally seen from afar—emphasizing the bleakness of his surroundings—and with the camera slightly above eye level. Scenes in the black-market nightclub are taken sensuously close, and often at waist level." Pabst also developed the technique of "editing on movement," whereby a performer begins a motion in one shot and continues it in the next; audiences, watching the movement, are unaware that two shots have been combined.

Another important German director of the twenties was Fritz Lang, a former architect whose films ranged from lavish interpretations of the Nibelungen legend to *Metropolis*, a chilling vision of life in the twenty-first century. In the latter, the city of the future is a multileveled tower in which the rich enjoy a life of luxury while the workers slave in subterranean dungeons. A plot to replace the slaves with mechanical robots is foiled, and at the end labor and capital join hands to make a better world. When the film was released in 1927, critic Robert E. Sherwood declared the plot ludicrous but admitted that "in all my years as a paid guest at movie palaces I have never seen such amazing pictures as are crammed into every reel of this gigantic production. Fritz Lang ... and Karl Freund, who commanded the battery of cameras, have combined to produce photographic effects that are not far short of miraculous."

A victim of its own success, the German film industry was pillaged by Hollywood, which was dazzled by the virtuosity of the German movies and could afford to pay irresistible salaries to the men who had made them. Lubitsch and Dupont, Murnau and Freund, Negri, Jannings, and countless others were wooed away by the American studios.

A similar fate befell the Swedes, who experienced a decade of notable cinema achievement between 1914 and 1924, at least in part because of their neutrality in World War I. Under the leadership of producer Charles Magnusson, the Swedish film industry nurtured two extremely gifted directors who made films of a uniquely Swedish character. Victor Sjöström—who was known as Victor Seastrom when he came to the United States in 1923 and who late in his life played the leading role in Ingmar Bergman's *Wild Strawberries*—specialized in slow-paced film sagas based on Scandinavian legends and literature. Nature was an almost mystical force in his films, which used the coldly beautiful Nordic landscape to brilliant effect. Mauritz Stiller, on the other hand, first made his mark with sophisticated comedies. He later turned, with notable success, to the type of poetic dramas that Sjöström was making. Like many of the films of Sweden's "golden era" of cinema, Stiller's most famous film, *The Story of Gösta Berling*, was based on a novel by Selma Lagerlöf. The tale of a handsome defrocked priest struggling against his own pride and the hypocrisy of his countrymen, the film contains many striking scenes, among them the hero's flight across ice in a sleigh to escape a pack of pursuing wolves. In the secondary role of a young Italian countess who loves the priest, Stiller cast an untried student from the Royal Dramatic Academy. It was Greta Garbo's first important role, and when Stiller was offered a Hollywood contract after the film's release, Louis B. Mayer signed up Stiller's discovery too. Ironically, Stiller's American career was short and unrewarding, whereas the incomparable Garbo went on to become the most memorable actress in screen history.

Another great Scandinavian-born film-maker was Denmark's Carl Theodor Dreyer, a peripatetic director who worked in Sweden, Germany, Norway, and France, as well as in his own country. It was in France that his most noted film, *The Passion of Joan of Arc*, was made with an international cast and crew in 1928. Depicting the final day of Joan's trial and her subsequent execution, the film consists almost entirely of gigantic close-ups of the actors, of weapons, religious symbols, and other objects. The performers used no makeup, and the harsh photography accentuated their facial imperfections. "By keeping the camera this close to his principals and their surroundings," Arthur Knight comments in *The Liveliest Art*, "Dreyer magnified them beyond human dimension, suggesting the monumentality first of his characters and, ultimately, of the trial itself. As the inquisition grows in intensity, tighter and tighter become the shots until, in the final hail of questioning, the camera swoops up to the huge mouths that fill the screen, and glimpses of Joan cowering under each new barrage, her hands over her ears, her great eyes flowing with tears. . . . Dreyer seems to have pushed the silent cinema to the very edge of its limitations."

It was in France that the movies first began to be regarded by intellectuals as a serious art form. Inspired by Louis Delluc, "the cinema's first true aesthetic theorist," clubs and societies devoted to the study of films were founded, establishing a tradition that still flourishes. Among the directors influenced by Delluc was the brilliant but erratic Abel Gance. His most notable film was *Napoléon*, an epic that was

The film renaissance that engulfed Western Europe after World War I was sparked by a clutch of talented German writers, directors, and producers—a list that included Carl Mayer, F.W. Murnau, G. W. Pabst, and Fritz Lang as well as Robert Wiene. Under their aegis, boldly conceived and daringly executed new films supplanted the tamer works of the prewar period. The poster below promotes the film Metropolis, *Lang's 1926 exercise in Orwellian futurism.*

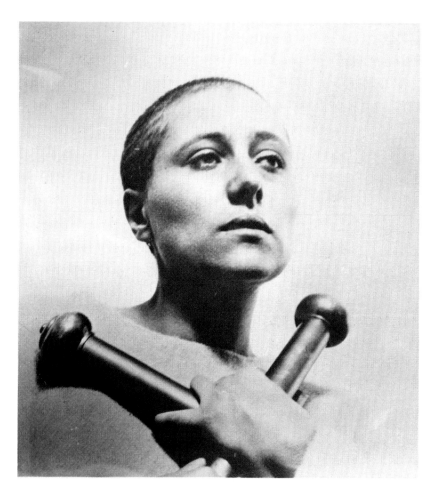

shown in 1926 on a triple screen, somewhat like the Cinerama of the 1950's. Sometimes Gance filled all three screens with a single panoramic view. At other times a triptych was created, as when a close-up of marching soldiers filled the center screen while long shots of the advancing army flanked it. "Gance," film critic David Robinson has written, "gave the camera a mobility and freedom it had not known before. He used dozens of cameras. ... He put cameras on automatic stands, on tracks, on dollies, on lifts, on guillotines, on special elevators, on stairways. He had cameras mounted on bicycles, on pendulums, on horseback; and he had little trucks like out-size roller skates. At a time when cameras were almost too heavy to lift, he introduced hand-held camera techniques. It was well over a quarter of a century before the camera was used again with such freedom; which explains why the French *nouvelle vague* was so exhilarated at the rediscovery of *Napoléon* when it was re-issued in Paris in the late fifties. Gance above all thought in images. He shattered the senses of his audience with pictures. Pictures already remarkable in themselves were hurled in torrents. They were cut with unprecedented rapidity, many shots lasting only a frame or two. They were superimposed and multiplied."

If *Napoléon* was ferociously inventive, René Clair's *The Italian*

German dominance of the international film market extended well into the 1920's, buoyed by the critical success of movies like The Last Laugh, *a Murnau–Mayer collaboration that contained a poignant performance by Emil Jannings (above) as an aged porter. The Germans' success naturally encouraged competition, and in 1928 Carl Theodor Dreyer, a Dane working in France, stunned audiences with* The Passion of Joan of Arc, *a film composed almost exclusively of compelling close-ups (opposite). This was also the golden age of Swedish cinema, and that nation's film legacy includes a number of movies directed by the legendary Mauritz Stiller. One of these,* The Story of Gösta Berling, *starred the young Greta Garbo (right).*

Straw Hat was an unadulterated delight. Based on a stage farce, it told the preposterous story of the misadventures of a bridegroom—en route to his own wedding—after his horse eats the hat of a lady who is embracing her lover. A duplicate of the hat must be found so that the lady's husband will not find out about her rendezvous, and the hero's wedding is, of course, long delayed by a sequence of absurd events. Clair's unfailing skill, wit, and timing make *The Italian Straw Hat* the most thoroughly enjoyable French film of the silent era.

Jean Epstein, Jean Renoir (son of the great painter), and versatile Jacques Feyder were other French directors working successfully in the twenties. It was two Spaniards, Luis Buñuel and the artist Salvador Dali, who made the most controversial "French" films of the era, however. Attempting to convert to celluloid the surrealist images of Dali's art, they collaborated first on *Un Chien Andalou*, which consisted of a series of deliberately shocking images. The opening sequence, in which

a man calmly slits a woman's eyeball with a razor blade, sets the tone for the film, which Dali said was intended "to plunge right into the heart of witty, elegant, and intellectualized Paris with all the weight of an Iberian dagger." The following year, 1930, Buñuel made *L'Age d'Or*, an equally outrageous film that was so blatant an attack on Catholicism and big business that riots broke out when it was shown in Paris.

Nowhere was the power of films to shock and proselytize realized more clearly than in Soviet Russia. "The cinema is for us," Lenin remarked, "the most important of the arts." The new Communist regime therefore gave its support to a flock of supremely talented young film-makers. Among the influential theorists teaching in the Russian schools of cinema were Lev Kuleshov and Vsevolod Meyerhold. Both made distinguished films themselves, but their influence on other directors was more important than their own accomplishments. Kuleshov believed that editing was the most important part of film-making, and he set out to prove his point by juxtaposing a single shot of an actor's face with three different close-ups: a bowl of soup, a dead woman in a coffin, and a child playing with a toy. "When we showed the three combinations to an audience which had not been let into the secret," recalled one of Kuleshov's students, "the result was terrific. The public raved about the acting of the artist. They pointed out the heavy pensiveness of his mood over the forgotten soup, were touched and moved by the deep sorrow with which he looked on the dead woman, and admired the light, happy smile with which he surveyed the girl at play. But we knew that in all three cases the face was exactly the same." Kuleshov also combined shots taken at different times and different places, splicing them together to show that films need not be bound by normal rules of chronology or geography. Meyerhold was less colorful but equally important. A former theater director who eschewed Stanislavskian naturalism, he constantly sought new forms and ideas, bringing to the cinema, as one historian has said, "his capacity for fundamental analysis of the nature and problems of a medium—the gift for asking the right questions."

French cinema was marked, almost from the outset, by a stylistic elegance and visual wit that awaited only the advent of sound to achieve full sophistication. Of early French film-makers, few are more honored today than René Clair, who wrote and directed a series of superb social satires—among them Le Quatorze Juillet, *opposite—in the late 1920's and early 1930's.*

Enormously influential too were the powerful newsreels compiled by Dziga Vertov, whose work foreshadowed the *cinema verité* of the 1960's. Preaching the supremacy of the documentary film, Vertov railed against acted cinema, which he regarded as false and nonrevolutionary. The theories of Vertov, like those of Kuleshov, Meyerhold, and others, were debated, discussed, and embellished by younger Russian film-makers. The greatest of these was Sergei Eisenstein, a former engineering student who turned first to the theater and then to films. Eisenstein came to believe that the key element in film-making was the juxtaposition of images in shocking ways, a technique designed to create new levels of meaning. In Japanese calligraphy, he pointed out, the symbol for heart and the symbol for dagger are combined to make up the symbol for sorrow. In the case of film, he insisted, the rapid juxtaposition of two disparate images can make them "explode" onto a new plane.

Eisenstein put this theory to work in *Potemkin*, the great silent film he directed in 1925. Commissioned to make a movie commemorating the abortive Russian revolt of 1905, he initially envisioned a film treating several separate incidents, among them the mutiny of the crew of the czar's battleship *Potemkin*. But when Eisenstein went to Odessa, the Black Sea port where the mutiny had occurred, and saw the long flight of marble steps on which the imperial troops had massacred a crowd of Russians during the mutiny, the sight so moved him that he decided to devote the entire film to the *Potemkin* episode.

The film's story is a simple one. The crew of the *Potemkin* is treated inhumanly and ordered to eat maggot-infested meat. They revolt, take over the ship, and sail into Odessa harbor. The people of the city gather on the steps to cheer them, but the czar's soldiers arrive and fire fusilade upon fusilade into the panic-stricken crowd, which flees down the steps, only to be trapped between the soldiers and mounted cossacks. The mutinous sailors aboard the *Potemkin* leave the port, expecting to be fired upon by the Russian fleet. But in the dramatic finale, the crews of the other ships disobey orders and allow the *Potemkin* to pass by.

The great scene on the steps best illustrates Eisenstein's genius:

> High on the steps, descending slowly in long, even lines, suddenly appear the soldiers in their white, immaculate tunics, splendid tall fellows, loading their rifles as they come. Every now and then the lines stop, fire, reload, descend again—nothing hurried, still nothing staged. And the steps below them, swept by that cold, casual rifle fire! A terror-stricken, bullet-stricken multitude, shorn in a breath of all enthusiasm, all revolutionary fire, resubmitting to the old tyranny—a mob, stumbling, falling, dodging, lying flat, rising again, pitching, huddling still, dwindling, fleeing, fleeing down those terrible, unescapable, everlasting steps, pursued grotesquely, almost humorously, by a bumping baby carriage bearing its unwitting infant, which has broken away from its mother's dying grasp. Most of this has been done by a swift, flickering assortment and throwing together of little pieces of pictures, a face here, a slipping body there, a flopping arm or leg, a pair of eye-glasses, a bit of torn clothing, a shuddering group or a convulsive body, as if the camera were dancing down the steps in that dance of death—as if the newsreel camera man were running about madly, stumbling and falling himself at times, but ever busy with his crank.

Wilton A. Barrett, the American critic who wrote the above description as part of his review of *Potemkin* in 1926, was stunned by the film's montage editing: "Perhaps the finest art yet put upon the screen has resulted, an art in its effect swifter, more inclusive, more accurate and absolute and directly expressive than the effect to be had from the sense of seeing itself. Is it the art of the motion picture, then, precisely this seeing of things for us beyond our own power of sight? Is it a synthesis of selected observations through the eye of the camera? Is it the director's function to study only reality in substance, form, and movement and then reproduce its essentials for us? ... POTEMKIN seems to tell us so."

Eisenstein's next film, *Ten Days That Shook the World*, was

"The cinema is for us the most important of the arts," Lenin declared—thereby giving sanction and impetus to Russia's nascent film industry. Predictably, many Soviet films of the Bolshevik era were graceless, labored tributes to the new regime, but the best consistently transcended mere ideology. One of these was Earth, *Alexander Dovzhenko's elegy to his native Ukraine and its people (above and left).*

another masterpiece. But because one of the film's heroes, Trotsky, had fallen from power, Eisenstein had to remake some episodes to eliminate the exiled leader from the action. From that point on, the director's relationship with the Soviet regime began to deteriorate. Charged with "formalism," Eisenstein was given few opportunities to use his enormous talent. Although he lived until 1948, he completed only six films after *Potëmkin.*

Almost equal in stature to Eisenstein, and far more prolific, was Vsevolod Pudovkin, a former chemist who became a film-maker after the overwhelming experience of seeing Griffith's *Intolerance.* A disciple of Kuleshov, Pudovkin stressed the importance of "plastic materials," objects that can be used imaginatively to help reveal the inner workings of a character. Pudovkin's most famous silent films were *Mother, The End of St. Petersburg,* and *Storm over Asia,* all of which glorified individuals who, after crises of conscience, acted on behalf of all the Russian people rather than in their own interests. Although he was a master of creative editing, Pudovkin never let technique overshadow the personal, moving stories that he told in his films. "Pudovkin's films resemble a song," one critic wrote, "Eisenstein's a shout."

Less well known, but highly respected by serious critics, are the films of a third Russian director, Alexander Dovzhenko, whose two major works, *Arsenal* and *Earth,* had their roots in the legends of his native Ukraine. "Both contain some of the most sensitive pictorial compositions the screen has ever known, superbly related in angle, tone, and movement," Lewis Jacobs, the American film scholar, has written. "So personalized are these pictures that they achieve the emotional intensity of great lyrical poems; so concentrated, rich, and unexpected are their images that Dovzhenko, perhaps more than anyone else, can be called the first poet of movies."

Because of their origins and political viewpoints, the films that emerged from Russia in the twenties often fell prey to Western censors, and their circulation was severely restricted. To Western filmmakers, however, the Russians' brilliance was readily apparent. "When the smoke of conflict had cleared away," Jacobs concluded, "it was apparent that a new era had begun in screen esthetics; a profound conception of film composition, consummating all the structural principles which had come down from Méliès, Porter, Griffith, and the other Europeans, had been formulated. With the Soviet films the art of movies became clarified."

A triumph of striking camera work and montage editing, Sergei Eisenstein's Potemkin must be ranked with the greatest movies ever made. Its climactic scene—the massacre at Odessa (below)—is intercut with sharply observed details, among them the death of a young woman (far left) and the subsequent headlong plunge of her baby's carriage (near left).

4

Heyday of Hollywood

IN HOLLYWOOD IN THE TWENTIES, as in the rest of Jazz Age America, "biggest" was synonymous with "best." Film companies merged, swallowed up competitors, and merged again until a handful of major studios controlled the business—which had become the nation's fifth-largest industry. Rival moguls bought up existing theaters and built ornate new ones, vying to see which company could control the largest chain of movie houses. They also vied for stars, paying enormous salaries to the lucky performers who were capable of attracting large audiences to the films they appeared in. Production budgets soared until the average five-reeler cost almost two hundred thousand dollars, and the spectacular *Ben-Hur*, released by Metro-Goldwyn-Mayer in 1926, cost a staggering six million. Larger budgets required more capital, which the banking interests of Wall Street happily supplied, becoming the true overlords of Hollywood in the process. There were plenty of profits for everyone in the early days, for by 1927 some sixty million Americans were going to the movies every week and the huge foreign market was hungry for Hollywood films.

Movies were no longer the entertainment of the lower classes alone; the great American middle class had finally embraced film, and it was they who filled the lavish movie palaces, decorated in Oriental, Moorish, or Baroque style and manned by platoons of uniformed ushers, which had proliferated across the nation. Intellectuals still scoffed at the movies, but Mr. and Mrs. America loved Hollywood's product.

What they loved most of all, evidently, were the daring, sexy films that purported to reflect the new morality of the roaring twenties. The studios presented an endless string of films about America's flaming youth, movies in which flappers and their boyfriends drove fast cars, used hip flasks, and participated in wild orgies—often with guests stripped daringly to their underwear—that lasted until dawn. Another type of film, pioneered by director Cecil B. DeMille, depicted beautiful young married women who were led, by boredom or frustration or both, to engage in extramarital affairs or to seek divorces but who usually wound up reunited with their original spouses. These DeMille creations, which bore such titles as *Don't Change Your Husband* and *Male and Female*, usually featured a scene in a fantastically ornate bathroom or bedroom where Gloria Swanson or some other leading lady was permitted to disrobe discreetly.

From sunrise to Sunset, Gloria Swanson was both a product and a prisoner of Hollywood's "star system." Presented to the moviegoing public as a kind of spangled Venus (opposite), the petite actress felt compelled to live the part, onstage and off. The result was an orgy of self-indulgence—led by Swanson and joined by countless other stars—that soon made Hollywood synonymous with extravagance.

The Ruritanian dramas written by Elinor Glyn, a novelist who enjoyed a considerable vogue in Hollywood in the twenties, dealt with royalty but shared the common preoccupation with sex. (Glyn is remembered today chiefly because she coined the phrase "It," meaning a certain indefinable kind of sex appeal.) In her biggest hit, *Three Weeks*, for instance, a young queen escapes from her loveless life for a brief period, during which a handsome commoner makes passionate love to her, first on a bed of roses and later on tiger skins. At the end of the three weeks she returns to her people, thoroughly satisfied by the romantic interlude. Similarly, the heroines of Rudolph Valentino's desert epics were very happy, despite initial struggles, to be abducted and seduced by the irresistible Latin lover.

It was all very titillating, and it was made even more so by the many stories that circulated about what actually went on in Hollywood. Everyone knew—or thought he knew—about the orgies and other wickednesses that were common in the film industry. This gen-

Cutthroat competition and systematic amalgamation reduced Hollywood's dozens of independent studios to a handful of all-powerful conglomerates by the end of the 1920's. Only the hardiest survived, and no one proved better at surviving than Louis B. Mayer, the head of M.G.M. A shrewd judge of talent, Mayer assiduously promoted the career of Irving Thalberg, the "boy wonder" of his production staff. In the photograph at left, Mayer (center) and Thalberg (right) hoist the key to success. To ensure outlets for their films, the major studios bought or built theaters across the country in the 1920's; and to attract patrons they decorated these pleasure domes in the most fantastic manner (right).

eral impression gained considerable credence when a series of scandals, trumpeted by the press, seemed to prove those stories true. First Fatty Arbuckle, the popular Sennett comedian, was charged with causing the death of a starlet at a wild party. Then director William Desmond Taylor was murdered and two actresses, lovely Mary Miles Minter and the screen's leading comedienne, Mabel Normand, were peripherally implicated. Later Normand's chauffeur was found murdered. No charges were ever pressed against either actress and Arbuckle was acquitted after three trials, but the careers of all three were ended. An even greater blow to Hollywood's image was the revelation that Wal-

lace Reid, a strappingly handsome actor who was one of the most popular leading men of the silent film era, was a drug addict; he died in a sanitarium in 1923.

Frightened by the indignant public's reaction to these scandals, Hollywood magnates hired Will Hays to serve as a sort of czar of industry morality. Hays saw to it that the stars were discreet about their vices and that films met certain moral standards. Under his stern aegis, sinning had to result in punishment or repentance; a character could enjoy a life of depravity as long as he met his comeuppance at the end of the movie. Hollywood's image was also improved by Cecil B. DeMille's expensive Biblical epics, *The Ten Commandments* and *The King of Kings*, which made even more money for the shrewd director than had his earlier melodramas of marital infidelity. Evidently the churchgoers of the nation were assuaged, for they continued going to the movies along with most other Americans.

To keep the nation's movie theaters, which numbered twenty thousand by 1926, supplied with new products, the big studios cranked out movies at a steady rate. Constantly increasing budgets and overheads meant that the sure thing—the formula film, the imitation of someone else's success—was favored over the fresh approach or the artistic gamble. Studio heads such as Louis B. Mayer and "boy genius" Irving

Working on a titanic scale, director Cecil B. DeMille (right) recreated Biblical Palestine and pharaonic Egypt in the California desert for The Ten Commandments. *There his construction crews erected the largest set Hollywood had ever seen —a pharaoh's palace guarded by five-ton stone sphinxes (below). DeMille's cast of thousands lived in a vast tent city nearby (left).*

Thalberg of MGM, Adolph Zukor and Jesse Lasky of Paramount, Carl Laemmle of Universal, William Fox, and the Warner brothers ruled their domains totally, and it was they who decided what should be filmed, how, and by whom. If they were displeased with a completed film, they ignored the director, recut the movie, and shot and inserted new footage. The final product in such cases often bore little resemblance to what the director had intended the film to be, but the studio heads' faith in their own ability to predict the public's taste was unequivocal, and no talent was great enough to awe them. Not even the classics were safe. When MGM made a film version of *Anna Karenina*, for instance, the studio entitled its vehicle for Garbo and John Gilbert *Love* and gave it a happy ending, one in which Anna, conveniently widowed, marries the faithful Vronsky and lives happily ever after.

Not surprisingly, many talented film-makers, especially those who had been wooed to Hollywood from Europe, found it impossible to work under such circumstances. Stiller, Dupont, and others returned home after disheartening experiences, and F. W. Murnau broke his contract after William Fox imposed happy endings on two of his films. Before his departure Murnau did manage to make one very fine movie, *Sunrise*, which was released in 1927. The story of a happily married rural couple whose lives are disrupted when he falls passionately in love with a vamp from the city, it is a lush and tender motion picture, one featuring superb camera work.

Victor Seastrom, the great Swedish director, toiled in the Hollywood vineyards for several years before returning to his native land. His two best American films starred Lillian Gish and were made at Metro. *The Scarlet Letter*, a faithful version of the Hawthorne novel, was highlighted by Gish's exquisite performance and by Seastrom's use

of natural beauty in contrast to the meanness of human bigotry. *The Wind*, not widely appreciated in its time, is regarded today as a masterpiece. Shot on location in the Mojave Desert, it uses the harsh Western landscape as the backdrop for its tale of a fragile girl from the East who is brutally treated by the family with whom she has come to live, forced into marriage with a boor, and driven to murder.

The one European who was able to forge a long, successful career in Hollywood was Ernst Lubitsch, who quickly established· his reputation as the director of witty, urbane, and commercially successful comedies. Strangely, it was Mary Pickford who brought him to California, a clear indication of her desire to broaden her range. Their film together was a flop, but *Marriage Circle*, a gay, sophisticated film about the extramarital adventures of two attractive couples, was a triumph for Lubitsch when it was released in 1924. So was *Forbidden Paradise*, which contains the famous scene in which Adolphe Menjou, as Catherine the Great's lord chamberlain, is confronted by a mob of revolutionaries. Reaching into his pocket for his pistol, Menjou pulls out his checkbook instead and ends the uprising that way. The scene is a prime example of Lubitsch's ironic, amusing approach, which was to reach full flower in the 1930's.

Perhaps the greatest, and surely the most undisciplined, of the European-born directors working in Hollywood in the twenties was Erich von Stroheim. Born in Vienna, Von Stroheim began appearing in American films as an extra in 1914, and he eventually became an assistant to D. W. Griffith. During World War I he became famous as "The Man You Love to Hate," playing villainous Prussians in a series of films. After the war, the bullnecked, monocled Austrian convinced Carl Laemmle of Universal to let him direct *Blind Husbands*, a film about adultery that shocked audiences with its realism and its message—that neglected wives are entitled to seek solace elsewhere. *Foolish Wives* was more of the same and was even more successful. Von Stroheim's extravagance in search of perfection was already becoming apparent, however, and his films were repeatedly over budget and overlong. When he directed *The Merry Widow* with Mae Murray and John Gilbert, he went so far as to order monogrammed silk underwear for the actors, even though the underwear would never be seen on the screen.

Von Stroheim's greatest accomplishment was *Greed*, his monumental film version of Frank Norris's novel *McTeague*. Nine hours long when it was completed, *Greed* was cut to four and a half at Irving Thalberg's insistence. The film was then taken out of Von Stroheim's hands and cut to two hours by MGM employees. The finished film, released in 1924, was an amputated version of what Von Stroheim had intended, but its brilliance is nevertheless apparent. *Greed* is the story of a boorish dentist, who is revealed to be practicing without a license, and of the greedy, penurious wife he eventually murders. All the ugliness and material lust of humankind is exposed. Von Stroheim, the master of detail, insisted on filming on location in San Francisco, in a

Lured to Hollywood by the prospect of great wealth and even greater artistic freedom, F.W. Murnau made only a few feature films before returning, disillusioned, to Germany. Written by Carl Mayer and entitled Sunrise, *Murnau's best American movie was a touching tale of infidelity and reconciliation (opposite). Swedish director Victor Seastrom's American career paralleled Murnau's, although he did labor in Hollywood for several years before retiring. During that time he produced one of the acknowledged classics of the silent screen,* The Scarlet Letter. *The still at right shows Seastrom with his Hester Prynne, actress Lillian Gish.*

house that had actually been owned by a man who had murdered his wife. A fight scene was filmed in Death Valley, under blistering heat that Von Stroheim felt enhanced the performances. Throughout, the actors were required to learn the script word by word, and retakes were made if they missed a word, even though the film was silent.

Von Stroheim's career as a director was brief: eight projects, the last in 1933, most of which he was not allowed to complete. In large measure his own perversity made him unemployable. Filming *Queen Kelly* with Gloria Swanson, for instance, he changed the story line during the course of shooting. When Swanson realized that the film could never be released due to its content—the Swanson character inherits a string of brothels—she walked out, forfeiting both her own money and that of her patron, Joseph Kennedy. Such episodes finished Von Stroheim's directing career, a tragic waste of enormous talent.

Equally out of place in Hollywood, although for different reasons, was Robert Flaherty, a mining engineer who won international recognition in 1922 with his memorable documentary *Nanook of the North*. Sponsored by a fur company, Flaherty spent months in the Arctic living with the Eskimos. The result was a poetic, moving film that was also a commercial success. Impressed, Jesse Lasky asked Flaherty to make a similar film in the South Seas. Refusing to work from a prepared

script, Flaherty spent more than three years filming *Moana*, which beautifully depicted the Samoans' day-to-day life. Paramount, disappointed at the lack of sex and the absence of epic confrontations between man and nature, nevertheless advertised the film as "the love story of a South Seas siren." Withdrawing in frustration from two subsequent Hollywood projects, Flaherty never again worked for an American studio, although this poet of the cinema remained active until his death in 1951.

Among those who were somehow able to survive within the studio system, and produce some fine films despite it, was King Vidor. Vidor, who had worked as a projectionist in a Texas nickelodeon while he was growing up, made his directorial debut in 1915, but his first success was

The Big Parade, an MGM blockbuster of a decade later. *The Crowd* (1928), the story of an average American couple trying to forge a life for themselves in a crowded and uncaring urban society, is judged by many to be Vidor's best silent film. The film is marked by uncompromising realism and by the director's own imaginativeness. Perhaps the most powerful scene is one in which the hero, made desperate by his child's illness, tries to quiet the people, trucks, and cars that are making noise beneath the youngster's window. The man, his arms upraised, moves through the crowd pleadingly, but the passersby are unconcerned about his sorrow.

Josef von Sternberg, a Vienna-born director who had come to America as a child, made a number of silent films that were distinguished, as Lewis Jacobs has observed, by "sensuous pictorialism." Von Sternberg's flair for composition, lighting, and photography is evident even in the poorest of his pictures, Jacobs comments, adding that his credo appears to be that "the movie is a painting in motion." His film *Underworld,* a realistic melodrama about Chicago gangsters, was an enormous hit in 1927. *The Docks of New York,* an excellent drama about New York's sordid waterfront denizens, and *The Last Command,* a film starring Emil Jannings as a White Russian exile earning his living by appearing as an extra in Hollywood films, served to further demonstrate the range and depth of Von Sternberg's art.

James Cruze, a director whose career as a whole was not especially distinguished, did create one superb film, *The Covered Wagon,* in 1922. Filmed in Nevada at a cost of $782,000, it was the first film to deal on an epic scale with the story of America's westward migration. Among the highlights were a buffalo stampede, an Indian attack on a wagon train, and a river-crossing by the wagons. Cruze was able to keep the stories of individuals in the forefront despite the spectacle, and the film was a huge success, playing more than a year on a reserved-seat basis in New York. Another classic Western was *The Iron Horse,* John Ford's film about the building of the Union Pacific Railroad. Other important directors of the twenties include Henry King, whose work ranged from the rustic *Tol'able David* to the soap opera *Stella Dallas;* William Wellman, who directed the aviation epic *Wings;* Tod Browning, who worked with Lon Chaney on many horror films; and Frank Borzage, who made two romances with Janet Gaynor and Charles Farrell, *Street Angel* and *Seventh Heaven.*

While these and other directors were winning plaudits, the man to whom they all owed so much was experiencing a tragic decline in his fortunes. D. W. Griffith had enjoyed a huge success in 1919 with *Broken Blossoms,* starring Lillian Gish as a cruelly mistreated waif and Richard Barthelmess as the Chinese man who loves her. It was, Lewis Jacobs notes, "a brilliant culmination for the 'sweet and innocent' era in American movies, already dying and being succeeded by the sophisticated, daring 'triangle era.'" *Way Down East* (1920), famous for its scenes of Gish leaping from ice floe to ice floe just a few feet from the edge of a gigantic waterfall, and *Orphans of the Storm* (1922) were both popular melodramas. But from that point on Griffith pleased neither critics nor public. Unable to cope with the new financial realities of big-business Hollywood, he was also loathe to eschew the sentimentality that was so out of fashion. When, desperate for income, he attempted to pander to public tastes by aping the successes of others, the results were disastrous. He worked only sporadically in the late twenties, and his last film was made in 1931. He lived in a rented room in Hollywood for seventeen more years and died in 1948, a bitter old man largely forgotten by the industry he had helped to create.

Forgotten too, by then, were many of the major stars of the silents, their careers terminated by the arrival of sound movies. "We didn't need voices," says Gloria Swanson, playing a reminiscing silent screen star in the 1950 film *Sunset Boulevard*. "We had faces then." Faces, and distinctive personalities, and talent, and enormous egos.

The selection of Swanson to play Norma Desmond in *Sunset Boulevard* was an inspired one, for no one more fully epitomized the silent screen star. A former notions-counter clerk from Chicago, Gloria Swanson progressed from Mack Sennett comedies to unchallenged supremacy on the Paramount lot. A diminutive woman with a superbly photogenic face, she was the heroine of those Cecil B. DeMille films about sophisticated married women in search of sexual fulfillment. At her peak, Swanson was earning twenty thousand dollars a week and spending most of it. When she liked a dress, she bought a dozen in different colors. When she traveled, it was in a private Pullman car, even if

Way Down East, which marked the apogee of D.W. Griffith's personal and professional fortunes, was released to universal acclaim in 1920. Filmed at considerable peril to both the director and his leading lady, Lillian Gish, this Victorian melodrama features a sequence in which Gish flees across an ice-choked river. At left, Griffith himself inspects the rolling rapids; at center, his star lies inert upon a floe—a scene captured on film by Griffith's long-time colleague Billy Bitzer. In the photograph at right, director and cameraman are seen during a shooting break.

she was penniless at the moment. When she married, it was to a European nobleman. Swanson was, in short, a star.

While Swanson played women of the world, Mary Pickford, who was five years older, still portrayed young heroines. Her fans knew that she and Douglas Fairbanks, who ruled Hollywood's social life from their hilltop mansion, Pickfair, had each divorced their spouses in order to marry one another. Nevertheless, every time Mary was cast as a mature, sophisticated woman, box-office receipts dropped ominously. *Little Lord Fauntleroy*, *Little Annie Rooney*, and similar films casting Mary as a plucky girl were what the fans wanted. When Pickford cut her long curls in 1928, there was extensive press coverage of the momentous event. But it was clear to everyone by then that the spectacle of a mature woman playing little girl roles was becoming almost grotesque. Wisely, "Little Mary" retired soon thereafter.

Fairbanks, on the other hand, was able to find a new image in the twenties. Sensing that his fans were becoming tired of his variations on the all-American hero, he switched to swashbuckler roles and won even greater popularity. In films such as *Robin Hood*, *The Thief of Bagdad*, and *The Mark of Zorro* he displayed a prowess at acrobatics that delighted his admirers.

The other top male star of the early twenties was Rudoph Valentino, an Italian immigrant who was earning his living as a tango dancer

"DOUGLAS FAIRBANKS AS THE GAUCHO"

United Artists Picture

in nightclubs when he was cast in MGM's *Four Horsemen of the Apocalypse*. Playing an Argentine playboy who becomes a hero in World War I, the swarthy Valentino overwhelmed female moviegoers, who quickly made it apparent to the studio bosses that a new star had been born. Films like *The Sheik, Blood and Sand*, and *The Son of the Sheik* made millions, though Valentino was a far from subtle performer. Men didn't care for him, evidently sensing something effete in the dashing actor who wore a slave bracelet presented to him by his wife and who was branded a "pink powder-puff" by a Chicago newspaper. Women, on the other hand, couldn't get enough of Valentino, and they envied his leading ladies—demure, virginal heroines who fought off Rudy's advances at first but soon returned his ardor. Valentino's death from peritonitis in 1926 set off an unprecedented orgy of grief. One hundred thousand women filled the streets outside the New York funeral parlor where their idol's coffin was on display and then filed weeping past his bier. Pola Negri, Valentino's alleged fiancée, arrived from California too late for the funeral but not too late for some highly dramatic mourning for the benefit of the press. And every year thereafter, on the anniversary of the actor's death, veiled mystery women would appear to place flowers on his grave. Valentino's popularity inspired numerous imitators, men like Ramon Novarro, Antonio Moreno, Ricardo Cortez, and other "Latin lovers," but no other actor ever received the intense adoration that Valentino had commanded.

She was Mary Pickford, "Little Mary" to legions of doting admirers. He was Douglas Fairbanks, the epitome of the matinee idol. And they (right) were Hollywood's royal couple, uncrowned but undisputed sovereigns of a never-never land they ruled from Pickfair, their hilltop mansion. When his career as the clean-cut hero of countless popular romances began to wane, Fairbanks turned to swashbucklers, playing the lead in such films as The Thief of Bagdad, Robin Hood, and The Gaucho (left). Pickford, on the other hand, was never able to escape winsome juvenile roles (below), which she played until she was well into her thirties.

Valentino's successor as the screen's leading lover was John Gilbert, an American who became a star in *The Big Parade*. Combining American vitality with European suavity, Gilbert set female hearts aflutter. His love scenes with Greta Garbo in three films were considered remarkably passionate in their day, and the rumors of an offscreen romance between the two only enhanced their popularity.

Garbo was the film sensation of the late twenties, outshining every other actress and becoming, in the process, the most legendary of all screen stars. Her image was that of the unattainable beauty who promises incredible sexual delights if only her aloofness can be overcome. When, for instance, John Gilbert embraces her against her will in *Love*, she does not fight him off; she simply stands there, cold and unresponsive. It is a chilling and totally effective rebuke. At a later point, however, her passion matches his, and she responds on this occasion with electrifying intensity.

Norma Talmadge, leading lady of the First National studio, specialized in playing heroines who aged during a film's progress. Married to producer Joseph Schenck, who nurtured her career, she is not well known today because many of her films have been lost. Nonetheless, she was one of Hollywood's top stars. Her sister Constance, also popular in the twenties, played vibrant, comic roles, but Norma's fans wanted to see her suffer—and suffer she did in such films as *The Sacrifice of Kathleen*, *The Branded Woman*, and *Love's Redemption*.

Another pair of sisters, Lillian and Dorothy Gish, had achieved stardom in D. W. Griffith's films. Dorothy was a charming comedienne; Lillian, an ethereally lovely woman, was regarded as the finest of all screen actresses. Her performance in Seastrom's *The Scarlet Letter* remains an impressive piece of acting, even after half a century. Critic

The silent screen was dominated by two sets of acting sisters, the Talmadges and the Gishes. Norma Talmadge (far left) was one of the era's greatest mimes, but her lamentable Brooklyn accent proved a severe disability after the advent of sound. Her sister Constance (seen at near left) enjoyed a long career in films, one that included a role in D.W. Griffith's Sunny. *Griffith worked with many Hollywood stars, but he is most frequently associated with Lillian and Dorothy Gish, seen at left in a still from* Orphans of the Storm. *The decade's most popular foreign-born stars were the Latin lover, Rudolph Valentino, waltzing at near right with Vilma Banky, and Pola Negri, shown at far right being coached by émigré director Ernst Lubitsch.*

Pauline Kael wrote in 1968 that "her Hester Prynne is one of the most beautifully sustained performances in screen history—mercurial, delicate, passionate. There isn't an actress on the screen today, and perhaps there never was, who can move like Lillian Gish; it's as if no bones, no physical barriers, stood between her intuitive understanding of the role and her expression of it." A lack of public enthusiasm for her films—coupled with Garbo's arrival at Metro, where Gish was under contract—effectively terminated her career as a leading lady.

Thoroughly unique was the appeal of Lon Chaney, the famous "man of a thousand faces." A master of grotesque makeup, he starred in such films as *The Phantom of the Opera* and *The Hunchback of Notre-Dame.* The son of deaf-mute parents, Chaney learned sign language and mime at an early age. As a result, he was a superb pantomimist and a brilliant actor, and he was able to convey character and win sympathy despite the hideous appearance that many of his roles required.

The preeminent cowboy star of the era was Tom Mix, who, like William S. Hart, had an authentic Western background. Unlike Hart, Mix starred in films that were unashamedly romantic and bore no relation at all to reality. A former sheriff and Texas Ranger, Mix did his own stunts on his famous horse Tony and he had a large, faithful following. Mix enjoyed the trappings of stardom and played the role to the hilt: he always wore a white suit in public, and atop his palatial home the name TOM MIX was spelled out in ten-foot neon letters.

Clara Bow, the famous "It" girl and the epitome of the screen flapper, also relished stardom. She loved to ride down Hollywood Boulevard in an open car, accompanied by several enormous dogs selected because their red fur matched her hair. "She danced even when her feet were not moving," Adolph Zukor later recalled. "Some part of her was in motion all her waking moments—if only her great rolling eyes." Miss Bow was the vivacious, good-hearted girl who flirted with fire and danced the nights away in *Dancing Mothers*, *The Wild Party*, and similar films. She evidently played as hard as she worked and paid the price in her later life, which she spent in a sanitarium.

Other major female stars of the decade were Pola Negri, who played

fiery, exotic heroines; Mae Murray, an eccentric blond who was famous for her "bee-sting" lips; Marion Davies, a charming comedienne whose career was advanced by her lover, William Randolph Hearst; Vilma Banky, a lovely Hungarian actress who made several romantic films with Ronald Colman; and Corinne Griffith, a dark-haired beauty billed as "the orchid lady." Notable male stars included John Barrymore ("the world's greatest actor as the greatest lover of the ages," trumpeted the ads for his film *Don Juan*), Thomas Meighan, Charles Ray, and Richard Barthelmess, the likable star of D.W. Griffith's last successes.

Today it is often hard to identify the singular appeal of many silent film stars, whose styles of acting often strike modern viewers as ludicrous. It is a far different story with silent comedy, however. The films of the great Hollywood comedians—Chaplin, Keaton, Harold Lloyd, Harry Langdon—are an enduring delight, probably the most lasting achievement of American silent films.

After turning to features in the early twenties, Chaplin made fewer and fewer films, sometimes taking years to produce a single movie. Almost without exception, these comic masterpieces were worth the wait. *The Kid*, in which the tramp adopts an abandoned child (Jackie Coogan) and later fights the authorities who want to take him away, and *The Circus*, featuring a sidesplitting tightrope sequence, were wonderful, but *The Gold Rush*, released in 1925, was superb. Nine reels long, it deals with Charlie's adventures in a Klondike mining camp: his search for gold, his attempt to win the affection of a local dance-hall girl, and his hilarious efforts to avoid being eaten by bears and by prospectors who are bigger and hungrier than he. The most memorable scene is one in which he dines on an old shoe. Chaplin's artistry turns the shoe into a gourmet feast: he carves it carefully, smacks his lips in anticipation, and then eats it with gusto and appreciation, sucking the nails as if they contained the most succulent juices and twirling the laces around his fork as if they were spaghetti.

The coat was too small, the pants too large, the moustache patently false—and the resultant silhouette (above) instantly recognizable wherever movies were shown. Charlie Chaplin's tramp spoke to all walks of life—and never more eloquently than in such silent films as The Kid *(opposite), which costarred Jackie Coogan, and* The Gold Rush, *whose memorable scenes include one in which Chaplin dines with exquisite grace and apparent relish upon a boiled shoe (right above).*

Chaplin's closest comic rival was Buster Keaton, whose best films, *The Navigator* and *The General*, are brilliant achievements. The son of vaudevillians, he was given the nickname Buster by the master magician Harry Houdini, a family friend, after Keaton fell downstairs at the theater when he was six months old. Young Keaton's natural acrobatic talent soon became obvious, and his parents began including him in their act, tossing him around like a human mop, much to their audiences' glee. In 1917 he joined Fatty Arbuckle's film troupe as a supporting player and quickly learned the rudiments of film technique. Two years later, producer Joseph Schenck set up a company for Keaton, who began by making his own two-reelers and in 1923 turned to feature films, becoming one of Metro's biggest attractions. Keaton was the master of the deadpan; "the great stone face" they called him, although he did show emotion in subtle ways, through his movements and in his remarkable eyes. He always played the stoic, battling stupid people and heartless machines, always coming out on top. No one who saw them can ever forget such marvelous scenes as the one in which Keaton stands proudly on the prow of a freshly christened ship that slides down the launching plank—and then continues down, down, down until the ship and Keaton are totally submerged. Equally memorable is the moment in *Steamboat Bill, Jr.* when the side of a house falls over on Keaton, who escapes unscathed because he happens to be standing on a spot that coincides with an open window. As James Agee has pointed out, Keaton was "the only major comedian who kept sentiment almost entirely out of his work, and he brought pure physical comedy to its greatest heights. Beneath his lack of emotion he was also subtly sardonic; deep below that, giving a disturbing tension and grandeur to the foolishness, for those who sensed it, there was in his comedy a freezing whisper not of pathos but of melancholia."

There was certainly no melancholia in the films of Harold Lloyd, who may have lacked the depth of Chaplin and Keaton but who was every bit as funny. Lloyd was working as an extra on the Universal lot when he met Hal Roach, who subsequently produced a series of one-reelers starring Lloyd as a character named Lonesome Luke, a frank imitation of Chaplin's Little Tramp. Later Lloyd was to develop his own character, that of a decent, optimistic, and eager young man who wore horn-rimmed glasses and always emerged triumphant from the incredible scrapes he got into. Sight gags were Lloyd's specialty, as *Safety Last*, his riotously funny film of 1922, was to prove. Playing a department store clerk who, through a combination of circumstances, is forced into posing as a professional "human fly," Lloyd climbs up the side of a tall skyscraper as traffic whizzes below. Audiences squealed with delight as Lloyd missed his footing and grabbed the hands of a huge clock—only to have the face of the clock open out, leaving Lloyd hanging in midair.

For a brief time, baby-faced Harry Langdon equaled the popularity of Chaplin, Lloyd, and Keaton. Coming to the movies at the age of forty after a long career in vaudeville, Langdon played the dim-witted innocent who was totally oblivious to the dangers that faced him but came out unscathed anyway. As Frank Capra, who directed many of

Langdon's films, recalled, "Chaplin *thought* his way out of tight situations; Keaton *suffered* through them stoically; Lloyd overcame them with *speed*. But Langdon *trusted* his way through adversities, surviving only with the help of God or goodness." A brilliant pantomimist, Langdon made the mistake of believing his reviews, which suggested that he was solely responsible for the brilliance of the vehicles in which he appeared. Loathe to share credit for his successes, he cut himself off from his key collaborators and soon found that his moment in the sun was over.

In 1927, Stan Laurel and Oliver Hardy, both veterans of Hal Roach comedy shorts, made the first of their countless films. Laurel, a British-born performer who had come to the United States with the same troupe of comedians that brought Chaplin to America, was the guiding talent behind the team's success. Their films were built around the classic confrontation between a fat, foolish bully—Hardy—and his thin, shy victim—Laurel. Beginning realistically, the Laurel and Hardy

The 1920's were halcyon years for cinema comedy, and the inspired products of that period are among the silent screen's finest offerings. These films include Harold Lloyd's droll masterpiece, Safety Last *(above);* The General *and* The Navigator, *both starring Buster Keaton (opposite); and dozens of short films featuring the mismatched comic duo, Stan Laurel and Oliver Hardy (right).*

movies usually wound up in hilarious mayhem involving the total destruction of a piano, car, or similar object and a slapstick climax that often featured custard pies.

Hollywood's golden age of comedy ended with the introduction of sound films, as did the careers of so many of its talented stars and directors. Succeeding generations of filmgoers have been introduced to the great comedians by showings at museums, on television, and at revival houses. As a result, Chaplin, Keaton, Lloyd, and Laurel were all personally honored in their old age at film festivals, Academy Awards ceremonies, and other similar functions around the world, small payment indeed for the enormous pleasure their films have given to so many.

WARNER BROS. SUPREME TRIUMPH
AL JOLSON
IN
"The JAZZ SINGER"

5

Film Finds Its Voice

"A MARVELOUS DEVICE known as the Vitaphone, which synchronizes sound with motion pictures, stirred a distinguished audience in Warners' Theatre to unusual enthusiasm at its initial presentation last Thursday evening," *The New York Times* informed its readers on August 7, 1926. "The natural reproduction of voices, the tonal qualities of musical instruments and the timing of the sound to the movements of the lips of singers and the actions of musicians was almost uncanny . . . . The future of this new contrivance is boundless. . . ."

The Vitaphone presentation that so impressed the *Times*'s film critic was not a feature-length "talkie" but rather a selection of short subjects that included a spoken introduction by Hollywood morals czar Will Hays and a series of musical performances by an orchestra, an opera star, and various instrumentalists. Not until a year later, on October 6, 1927, did *The Jazz Singer*, the first feature film to use recorded songs and a few lines of dialogue, open on Broadway. "You ain't heard nothin' yet!" the film's star, Al Jolson, declared before bursting into song. His words were more prophetic than he could have guessed, for from that moment the silent film was a moribund art form.

The Hollywood studios had been extremely reluctant to introduce talking films. The public was perfectly happy with silents, and the cost of converting theaters and studios to sound was prohibitive. Well satisfied with the status quo, movie moguls had spurned all offers concerning talkies. It was only because the Warner brothers were in desperate financial straits—they were unable to buy enough theaters to guarantee outlets for their films—that they decided to buck the trend and put every nickel they could into the Vitaphone process. *The Jazz Singer* quickly proved them right, as sound transformed their struggling company into a prosperous major studio.

The technological breakthrough had come years before and many short talking films had already been released, but it remained for The Jazz Singer, *issued in 1927, to call public attention to the possibilities of sound. Al Jolson's prophetic line—"You ain't heard nothin' yet!"—sent shock waves through the film industry, which suddenly realized that it could no longer forestall the coming of the "talkies."*

Like the invention of the cinema itself, the early history of sound films is a welter of conflicting claims. One thing is clear, however: sound reproduction intrigued film-makers from the very beginning, and several pioneers in the field did produce talking short subjects. Early in this century, for instance, Sarah Bernhardt and other French stars had appeared in talking films of less than a minute's duration, but the sound in those and similar efforts was extremely primitive. It remained for Lee de Forest, an American inventor, to solve one of the key problems: how to amplify recorded dialogue and music so that it

could be heard throughout a theater. With this accomplished by the end of World War I, De Forest began working on a process that would record sound not on discs but on movie film itself. By 1923, talking short subjects produced by De Forest were playing in a number of American theaters.

Interestingly enough, the process eventually adopted by the Warners was not De Forest's sound-on-film system. Instead, they chose Bell Telephone's Vitaphone process, which recorded sound on discs that were synchronized with the film. After the success of *The Jazz Singer*, Fox began producing a series of Movietone shorts using another sound-on-film system, and in future years a series of law suits were launched by those who claimed ownership of various rival processes. Eventually, one of these sound-on-film systems was adopted universally. Audiences couldn't have cared less whether the sound was recorded on film or discs, of course; all they knew was that sound vastly enhanced their enjoyment of movies.

The first all-talking feature was an abominable film called *Lights of*

"Garbo talks!" the advertisements trumpeted—and talk she did, in a lush, mellifluous, deeply accented voice that only enhanced her already considerable reputation. The film was Anna Christie (right), and the line was a throwaway, but the effect was galvanic; Garbo fans were ecstatic. Audiences reacted less charitably to Garbo's costar, John Gilbert (above), whose light tenor voice seemed ludicrously ill-matched with his aquiline good looks, making him the most celebrated casualty of the conversion to sound. Garbo's career was also truncated—but by her own choice, and not before the camera's flattering eye (left) had made her a living legend.

New York, released by Warners in 1928. It cost seventy-five thousand to produce and grossed four million, thereby convincing all remaining skeptics that sound films were what the public wanted. Borrowing vast sums—and in the process consolidating Wall Street's hold over Hollywood—the studios frantically converted their stages and theaters to sound. In an attempt to salvage their inventory of completed silents, they added songs and irrelevant talking episodes, hoping that such measures would temporarily satisfy the public. By 1929, 75 percent of the nation's theaters were equipped for sound, and by 1930 the conversion was complete.

In the process, once flourishing careers came to a screeching halt. Stars with foreign accents, lisps, or nasal twangs quickly disappeared. ("One of the revelations of the talkies," commented *The New York Evening Post*, "is the fact that the most beautiful nose in the world isn't much of an asset to an actress if she talks through it.") John Gilbert, the silent screen's most popular leading man at the time, is perhaps the prime example of an actor who became a liability rather than an asset to his studio when his speaking voice failed to please the public.

Studios used the conversion to sound as an excuse to jettison many high-priced stars whose voices were not really bad but who had simply been around too long. Hollywood wanted new faces, performers who had been trained in the theater and knew how to speak dialogue. Broadway stars such as Helen Hayes, Ruth Chatterton, and Jeanne Eagels suddenly found themselves in great demand in Hollywood. And so did numerous young players imported from New York, among them Claudette Colbert, Clark Gable, Spencer Tracy, James Cagney, Bette Davis, Barbara Stanwyck, Paul Muni, Edward G. Robinson, and Fredric March, all of whom were to become major stars. Charlie Chaplin simply ignored sound and continued making silent films throughout the thirties. As for Garbo, she made a delayed but triumphant sound debut in 1930's *Anna Christie* ("Garbo talks!" the ads trumpeted.) "Give me a whiskey with ginger ale on the side, and don't be stingy, baby" were her first screen words, delivered in a husky, heavily accented voice that was eminently suitable to the love-starved, doomed heroines she played.

Like everyone else in Hollywood, the stars found themselves being ordered about by a new phenomenon on the movie scene: the sound engineer. Because the cameras used at the time were very noisy, they had to be confined to soundproof booths. This resulted in the total elimination of camera mobility. Similarly, microphones had to be hidden in potted plants or other props and the actors were obliged to speak directly into them. Like the camera, the performers were thereby sorely restricted in their movements. These early mikes were also very sensitive, picking up every minor sound. If the script called for a letter to be opened, for instance, the letter had to be dampened beforehand lest the microphone amplify the crackling of the paper. Rustling materials such as taffeta could no longer be used for costumes. Gone too were the days when the director could give instructions to the actors during the shooting of a scene, and the use of mood music to inspire the performers also became a luxury of the past. The result of all this was a series of static, dialogue-heavy versions of stage plays and a rash

Unflinchingly graphic and unwaveringly romantic, All Quiet on the Western Front *(above) is perhaps the finest antiwar film ever made. Its sentiments so incensed members of the newly formed Nazi party that they took to sabotaging screenings of the 1930 film by releasing snakes and rats in the theaters where it was playing. Equally controversial, although for very different reasons, was King Vidor's* Hallelujah! *(right). Considered tame—even retrograde—today, this ambitious overview of black America was deemed needlessly provocative when the film was first released in 1929.*

of uninspired musical revues. The critics were horrified and mourned the demise of the silents.

It was not long, however, before solutions were found for the various technical problems, and a number of astute directors soon began to demonstrate how sound could be an invaluable asset in film-making. One such director was King Vidor, whose *Hallelujah!*, released in 1929 by MGM, was considered unique because it attempted to deal honestly with the experiences of black Americans. In actuality the film did little more than perpetuate well-established racial stereotypes, but Vidor's mastery of his craft is apparent, nonetheless, and his use of sound is unusually skillful for the period. Key scenes were shot on location in

the South without sound; dialogue was later recorded and synchronized with the actors' lip movements, an enormously difficult and tedious process at that time. In Vidor's hands, song and sound became intrinsic film elements, heightening the dramatic effect. And for the film's climax, a chase through an ominous swamp, Vidor devised a new approach. "Never one to treat a dramatic effect literally," he has said, "the thought struck me—why not free the imagination and record this sequence impressionistically? When someone stepped on a broken branch, we made it sound as if bones were breaking. As the pursued victim withdrew his foot from the stickiness of the mud, we made the vacuum sound strong enough to pull him into hell. . . ."

Another notable film that year was Rouben Mamoulian's *Applause*, in which Helen Morgan portrayed an aging burlesque star whose sordid existence and concern for her daughter drive her to suicide. Refusing to limit camera movement because of sound, the Armenian-born director mounted the booth containing the camera on wheels so that it could be moved about. Mamoulian also insisted on using two cameras to increase the number of possible angles. To this he added superimposition of sound tracks: a song from one scene was continued into the next but softened so that a conversation could be heard above it.

A third innovative director was Ernst Lubitsch, whose early sound musicals were enchanting entertainments. *The Love Parade* featured Jeanette MacDonald and Maurice Chevalier as a pair of royal lovers. Like Vidor, Lubitsch shot some scenes in silence and added sound later, thereby achieving maximum camera mobility. Throughout the film, he used sound both cleverly and irreverently. When the royal couple sing of their love, for instance, their servants parody them in a simultaneous

duet. Later a dog barks an echoing reprise of another song. Booming cannons disturb the lovers on their wedding night and when Chevalier tells a risqué story, a slamming door obliterates the punch line. The critics adored *The Love Parade*, and they were even more enthusiastic about Lubitsch's next film, *Monte Carlo*. The highlight of that 1930 production was a sequence in which Jeanette MacDonald, fleeing from her rich but repulsive husband, escapes on a train called the Blue Express. The sound of the train's wheels gaining speed leads into the opening bars of a song, "Beyond the Blue Horizon," which MacDonald sings as the train hurtles through the countryside. This type of "sound montage" was totally new and extraordinarily effective.

The most highly praised American drama of the early talkies period was Lewis Milestone's unforgettable antiwar film, *All Quiet on the Western Front*. This story of a young German soldier exposed to the horrors of a World War I battlefield would have been memorable even if it had been shot, as originally intended, as a silent film; sound only

Two of the towering geniuses of German cinema, joined by an all but unknown starlet, produced one of the enduring classics of movie history in 1929. The film was The Blue Angel, *and it was directed by Josef von Sternberg. In it, Emil Jannings plays a love-besotted pedant (opposite), and Marlene Dietrich an amoral showgirl. Audiences on both sides of the Atlantic were mesmerized by the film's aura of decadence and bewitched by Dietrich's rendition (above) of "Falling in Love Again."*

Overleaf: Hollywood soon spawned a brand of literature all its own—the movie magazine. By the 1930's this ancillary industry was peddling its gaudy wares from magazine racks in every country in the world.

served to enhance it. When, for instance, Milestone intercut film footage of soldiers running across the field and still shots of a machine gun emplacement, it was the cacophony of gunfire that unified the sequence. And the poignant climax, in which the young soldier rises from his trench in an attempt to catch a butterfly and is shot down by the enemy, is made all the more moving by the sound of a harmonica being played softly in a nearby trench. For its foreign releases, *All Quiet on the Western Front* was dubbed in various languages. Until then Hollywood had been making different versions of its talkies, using German-speaking actors, for example, to film a scene after the American performers had finished.

Like their American counterparts, European audiences expressed a strong preference for talking films. And like the first American attempts, the initial European talkies were crude and static. In France, however, René Clair showed his colleagues that sound could be used gracefully and effectively. His charming musical film, *Sous les Toits de Paris*, is opened by a street singer whose song is joined, one by one, by all the neighborhood residents and shopkeepers as Clair's camera wanders down the street, entering various shops and windows in a quick and entertaining way to introduce all the film's characters. "Rather than follow the sound engineer's advice," Clair recalled in later years, "and plant a mike beside everybody, which they would have to turn on and off so as to get the sound of a voice fading as the camera moved on ... I attached the mike to a movable pole. At the time, to move the mike was blasphemous. It stood still, and *you* had to move around it. We did it my way, and the result was perfect."

In Germany, the only Western European nation that had patented its own sound-on-film system and did not have to pay royalties to America, producers cranked out innumerable operettas, most of no critical consequence. It took a film of the caliber of Joseph von Sternberg's *The Blue Angel*, released in 1929, to restore the German film industry to world prominence. Invited to come to Germany by Emil Jannings, whose own Hollywood career was ended by sound, Von Sternberg created a masterful film out of the story of a respected professor who becomes infatuated with an immoral cabaret singer. Jannings gave a fine performance in the leading role, but it was Marlene Dietrich who stole the film with her portrayal of Lola, the girl who used sex to achieve her goals. Dressed in top hat, brief costume, and long stockings held up by garters stretching across naked thighs, she sang "Falling in Love Again" and exuded a sexuality that no language barriers could obscure. Von Sternberg returned to Hollywood in triumph, bringing the fabulous Dietrich with him.

The films of Lubitsch, Mamoulian, Vidor, Milestone, Clair, and Von Sternberg were convincing proof that sound movies could equal, and indeed surpass, the artistry of the silents. By 1931 all but the most die-hard advocates of silents acknowledged that films were entering a new era of unlimited potential. "I have never since re-discovered," Clair has said, "the joy and excitement that we (the crew) had at the beginning of sound, when everything was being discovered. We were lucky to be working at that time."

PHOTOPLAY

The National Guide to Motion Pictures

January 1926

25 cents

SCREENLAN

Norma Shearer's RING

MOTION PICTUR

AUGUST - 25 CTS

Do You Believe in Fortune Telling?

Hollywood Great Love S

CINEMA

THE MAGAZINE OF THE PHOT

PHOTOPLAY

DECEMBER

The Beauty Who Sits Alo

CLASSIC

JULY   25¢

A BREWSTER PUBLICATION

MOTION PICTUR

DECEMBER - 25 CTS   A BREWSTER MAGAZINE

Fighting the Lean Years

PHOTOPLAY

Whose Heart is Whose in Hollywood

PHOTOPLAY

The National Guide to Motion Pictures

FEBR

"When Ten Cents Was Big Money"

The New and Amazing Diary of a Star

How To Hold Your You

ON PICTURE
CLASSIC
25

PICTURE PLAY
NOV. 1927
LITTLE JOURNEYS TO FILMLAND

The Truth About Salar

CINEMA
THE MAGAZINE OF THE PHOTOPLAY

ON Picture
25 CENTS

The Talkies'
First Birthc

The National Guide to Motion Pictures
PHOTOPLAY
October 1924

A BREWSTER PUBLICATION
MOTION PICTURE
MAGAZINE
THE QUALITY MAGAZINE OF THE SCREEN
DECEMBER
25

Ramon Novarro

N PICTURE
MAGAZINE OF THE SCREEN
MAGAZINE
Shilling

The World's Leading Moving Picture Magazine
PHOTOPLAY
April
The Studio Secret
The Tragedies of Pauline Frederick

A BREWSTER PUBLICATION
MOTION PICTURE
MAY
MAGAZINE
25

Gloria Swanson

VALENTINO'S HOLLYWOOD LIFE

6

Chorines and Comics, Cowboys and Crooks

"FOR ALL THEY THAT TAKE THE SWORD shall perish with the sword." That Biblical admonition appeared on the screen at the start of *Little Caesar*, the first in a series of violent films about gangsters that emanated from Hollywood in the early 1930's. Starring Edward G. Robinson as Rico, a ruthless hoodlum who rises to the top ranks of organized crime and winds up riddled with police bullets, Mervyn LeRoy's film took full advantage of sound. The crackle of gunfire, the wail of sirens, the screech of brakes, and the tough underworld slang that permeated the dialogue all added immeasurably to the film's impact.

The enormous popularity of *Little Caesar* and other sound films enabled Hollywood to sail smoothly through the early months of the Depression; in fact, film attendance in the United States rose to a new weekly high of 110 million in 1930. The industry eventually fell prey to the economic chaos that had already engulfed most of the nation's economy, however. Weekly movie attendance sank to sixty million in 1932 and plummeted even lower the following year. A partial recovery occurred at mid-decade, but by the end of the thirties movie theaters were offering double features, free dishes, and cash prizes in an attempt to recapture a dwindling audience.

More than ever the major studios imitated the successes of their colleagues; when one company hit upon a lucrative idea, a cycle of similar films poured out of Hollywood. *Little Caesar*, for example, spawned scores of undistinguished gangster movies and only a few good ones. *Scarface* was lifted above the norm by the skillful direction of Howard Hawks and by Paul Muni's powerful performance as an Al Capone-like gangster. *Public Enemy*, directed by William Wellman, was perhaps the best of the lot. Advertised as "the biography of a criminal," it catapulted cocky, magnetic James Cagney to stardom. Unlike most of the other films in the genre, *Public Enemy* made an effort to show the sort of social and economic conditions that produce criminals. In the course of the film Cagney climbs from petty crookdom to the top—a world of fast women, custom-made suits, and fancy cars—before meeting a violent death. The film's most famous scene is one in which Cagney, bored by his mistress's nagging at the breakfast table, shoves a grapefruit in her face.

The gangster genre came to an end because of public protests that American youth were being harmed by films glorifying violence and criminals. There were always new cycles ready to replace the old,

Hollywood's antidote to the Great Depression was escapist fantasy: a Busby Berkeley world of outsized sound stages, prancing chorines, and tinseled sets. Ostensibly, Hollywood moguls offered the urbane elegance and insouciant charm of performers like Fred Astaire and Ginger Rogers as a palliative to hard times. In the process, of course, they hoped to lure patrons back to their half-empty theaters.

however. In the so-called confession films, for instance, actresses such as Constance Bennett and Norma Shearer sinned, suffered, and then found tearful redemption in the arms of an understanding man. A cycle of horror films in the early thirties made legends of Boris Karloff and Bela Lugosi, who were known for the rest of their lives as Frankenstein and Count Dracula. Biographies of famous people were another successful genre. English actor George Arliss won critical acclaim for his depictions of various historic personages, although as writers Richard Griffith and Arthur Mayer point out, Arliss's heroes "all were crafty but benevolent old 'gentlemen who spent most of their time uniting unhappy young lovers." Later in the decade, Warners starred Paul Muni in two effective biographies, *The Story of Louis Pasteur* and *The Life of Emile Zola*.

Hollywood's primary message during the Depression years was that capitalist virtues—hard work, optimism, patriotism—were the answers to the nation's distress and that anyone espousing Communism or revolution was a dupe of sinister forces. Nevertheless, a number of powerful "message films" dealing with social problems were released in the 1930's. In *I Am a Fugitive from a Chain Gang*, directed by Mervyn LeRoy, Paul Muni played an unemployed war veteran who was framed for a crime he didn't commit and subjected to the horrors of a Southern prison. And Fritz Lang, who had emigrated to Hollywood from Nazi Germany, presented a chilling picture of mob violence in *Fury*,

Prohibition and public curiosity combined to create a new film genre in the early 1930's—the so-called gangster movie. The first of these to enjoy widespread popularity was Little Caesar, which was released in 1930, one year after the Saint Valentine's Day Massacre. Its star was Edward G. Robinson (near right), a square-faced, tough-talking cinema Capone who made dozens of derivative gangster movies (above) in the years that followed. Indeed, Little Caesar triggered uncounted gangland epics, the most successful of which was The Public Enemy. In that movie's most famous scene (far right), punk hood James Cagney demonstrates his complete contempt for his mistress (Mae Clark) by shoving half a grapefruit in her face.

released in 1936. Lang's star, Spencer Tracy, was superb as a hard-working gas station attendant who is arrested and charged with kidnapping while driving through a small town. Hysteria mounts as fear and ignorance transform supposedly righteous citizens into an angry mob. The sheriff is assaulted and the jail set aflame as the townspeople, their blood lust satisfied, watch the building burn. At a time when there were more than one hundred lynchings a year in the United States, *Fury* was remarkable for its outspokenness.

Like Lang, John Ford was able to rise above the restrictions of the studio system to create important, meaningful films. Interviewed in 1936, he bemoaned a system under which a director was assigned to a picture without even being asked how he felt about the material and without being given sufficient time for preparation. Scripts, often the work of a dozen different writers, were prepared to please the studio heads, not the directors, and the final cutting of most films was done without the director's participation. "It's a constant battle to do something fresh," Ford said. "They want you to continue whatever vein

you succeeded in with the last picture. You're a comedy director, or a spectacle director, or a melodrama director. . . . Another time they want you to knock out something *another* studio's gone and cleaned up with." Even for such towering talents as Lubitsch, Lang, Mamoulian, Von Sternberg, and Ford, a combination of compromise, determination, and deceit was required if a director was to exert any control over the final content of his films.

Ford, for instance, learned to use film so economically—to cut while filming—that the movies he made could not be put together by

others in a way that altered his own vision of the film. According to Richard Schickel, Ford's first masterpiece, *The Informer*, was filmed behind the studio's back in 1935. RKO had told Ford that Liam O'Flaherty's novel about a member of the Irish Republican Army who informs on a friend for a mere twenty pounds was not suitable movie material. Undeterred, Ford made the film in a studio annex in three weeks at a cost of less than $220,000. The result was a superior psychological drama, with Victor McLaglen giving the performance of his career as Gypo Nolan, the hulking dullard who impulsively betrays a friend in order to earn passage money to America. Filmed with a minimum of dialogue and with imaginative use of lighting and sound—the threatening tap of a blind man's cane, the relentless ticking of a clock—*The Informer* revealed Ford's unparalleled ability to create mood and sustain interior tension.

Dudley Nichols, the scriptwriter on *The Informer*, also wrote *Stagecoach*, Ford's classic 1939 Western that made John Wayne a star after ten lean years in Hollywood. Ford filmed the story, which involves a coachful of disparate passengers led by Wayne as the Ringo Kid, in Utah's magnificent Monument Valley. "His characters respond to this environment," author Peter Cowie writes, "drawing from it a kind of nobility that—in a crisis—enables them to act beyond their reputations. ... Ultimately, it is the visual communication of speed and danger that distinguishes *Stagecoach*: the high shots of the stage moving away unprotected across the vast salt flats; the stirring race against the Indians; the arrival of the cavalry."

Indisputably the most popular and durable of all film genres is the Western, which has undergone endless transformation since the heyday of William S. Hart and "Bronco Billy" Anderson. Stagecoach (left above), John Ford's 1939 classic, is one of the genre's archetypes. Appropriately, it made a star of John Wayne, who has subsequently become the quintessential Western hero. Destry Rides Again (opposite), which was also released in 1939, burlesqued the very values that Stagecoach espoused—and proved in the process that the genre could easily accommodate parody.

Other outstanding Westerns of the thirties were *Cimarron*, a story of the Oklahoma land rush; *The Virginian*, with Gary Cooper; and *Destry Rides Again*, a spoof in which James Stewart appears as a non-violent sheriff and Marlene Dietrich as a dance-hall girl. The last movie's most famous scene finds Dietrich engaged in a knock-down, drag-out fight with another actress; the scene ends when Stewart throws a bucket of water on the battling women. The role, a delightful departure for Dietrich, stood in sharp contrast to the exotic, untouchable creatures she had been playing in Josef von Sternberg's films.

Another blond sex symbol of the thirties was Mae West, whose 1932 debut provoked the wrath of various church groups, which were already concerned about the violence and sex in Hollywood films. West wrote most of her own dialogue, and much of what she wrote was tart and explicit. "I used to be Snow White, but I drifted," she remarked in one film, and when her jewels were admired in another— "Goodness, what beautiful diamonds!"—Mae retorted: "Goodness had nothing to do with it." Her pointed invitation, "Come up and see me some time," was often quoted. Mae didn't walk, she undulated. She didn't speak, she purred her lines in a way that inspired countless mimics. Two films, *She Done Him Wrong* and *I'm No Angel*, made her Paramount's top attraction and led to the creation of the Legion of

MAE WEST

"I'm No Angel" with CARY GRANT DIRECTED BY WESLEY RUGGLES

a Paramount Picture

Decency and the adoption of a tougher Production Code under Will Hays. Gradually, the spontaneity and spice were removed from Mae's films, and her flamboyant dialogue was bowdlerized.

Fearing further criticism, Hollywood in the mid-1930's turned from sex to so-called "family pictures." Many of the latter were dull and pretentious, but some were good entertainment. Among the best were two David O. Selznick productions, *Little Women* with Katharine Hepburn as a vivacious Jo, and *David Copperfield* with W. C. Fields as Mr. Micawber. Both were the work of George Cukor, one of the most talented of Hollywood's directors. For independent producer Samuel Goldwyn, William Wyler directed critically acclaimed versions of Emily Brontë's *Wuthering Heights*, with Merle Oberon as Cathy and Laurence Olivier as a brooding Heathcliff, and Sinclair Lewis's *Dodsworth*, starring Ruth Chatterton and Walter Huston. Moviegoers of all ages loved *Mutiny on the Bounty*, which starred Clark Gable as a dashing Fletcher Christian and Charles Laughton as a memorably malevolent Captain Bligh.

One wholesome genre that found new favor around 1933 was the musical. Sated by the deluge of all-singing, all-dancing films that had followed the introduction of sound in 1929, the public had shown little interest in such films for years. But in the mid-thirties the musical made a remarkable comeback. MGM offered tap-dancing Eleanor Powell and

Mae West's brand of brazen humor and sloe-eyed seductiveness titillated audiences in the early thirties. Many saw her flamboyance as a welcome alternative to the prim pretentiousness of most Hollywood films, but a powerful few did not. And thus, within months after the release of her first feature film, the Legion of Decency was formed to protect moviegoers from such innuendo-laden West vehicles as I'm No Angel *(above). Instead, audiences were proffered such saccharine works as* The Little Colonel, *whose child star, Shirley Temple (right), radiated wholesomeness.*

the team of Jeanette MacDonald and Nelson Eddy, who yodeled their way through a series of lavishly produced and rather witless operettas. Paramount capitalized on Maurice Chevalier, Mae West, and, later in the decade, Bing Crosby, the crooner who became America's favorite singing performer. Columbia had Grace Moore, one of the many opera stars who attempted to build screen careers, and Universal was literally saved from bankruptcy by the films of pretty Deanna Durbin, a teen-ager with a lovely soprano voice, natural beauty, and an easy charm. At Twentieth Century-Fox, blond Alice Faye headed the cast of many successful musicals. Topping them all was Shirley Temple, the little girl with the big curls, deep dimples, and pert if somewhat artificial manner who so appealed to the public that Fox thought it well worth their while to pay her three hundred thousand per picture. From 1934, when she was six, to 1939, Shirley ranked among the top box-office attractions in the nation. Usually playing an orphan in search of parents, or a child with only one parent in search of a second, she solved everybody's problems by dint of her ingenuity and perpetual optimism. Far more talented was Judy Garland, who became a star in 1939 in *The Wizard of Oz*, for which Shirley had been MGM's first choice.

Warner Brothers' contribution to the musical genre was a series of so-called "backstage musicals," many of which were choreographed by Busby Berkeley. The most famous of these films was *42nd Street*, the prototype for scores of others. It presents the story of a dedicated cast of actors rehearsing for a Broadway opening. Just before opening night, the star breaks a leg. All seems hopeless until someone suggests that a raw young girl from the chorus line be given the leading role. "You're going out a youngster," the director tells the chorine after a brief rehearsal, "but you've *got* to come back a star!" Needless to say, chorine Ruby Keeler does find stardom; she also finds love in the person of Dick Powell.

Berkeley's inventiveness never seemed to flag. In *Gold Diggers of 1933* he had one hundred blonds playing one hundred white pianos that danced (courtesy of one hundred men hidden underneath). Women transformed into human harps, hoofing on giant typewriter keyboards, in all sorts of extravagant costumes, dancing against all sorts of unlikely backgrounds and photographed from all sorts of unexpected angles— these were the Berkeley production numbers.

"Can't act. Slightly bald. Can dance a little." So read the report on Fred Astaire's screen test—surely one of the least perceptive evaluations in movie history. The Nebraska-born dancer had been a theater star in partnership with his sister Adele, and it was only after she married in 1932 that Astaire turned to films. He was, to be sure, skinny, egg-headed, and not terribly sexy. He was, however, the epitome of grace, elegance, and precision, and when he danced he was irresistible. RKO paired him with pretty Ginger Rogers, who had been playing wise-cracking chorines. On screen with Astaire, she was smart, sassy, and thoroughly appealing. "He gave her class, she gave him sex appeal," someone said, and the evaluation was correct.

Rogers and Astaire made nine films together during the thirties and endeared themselves to a generation. They danced together with con-

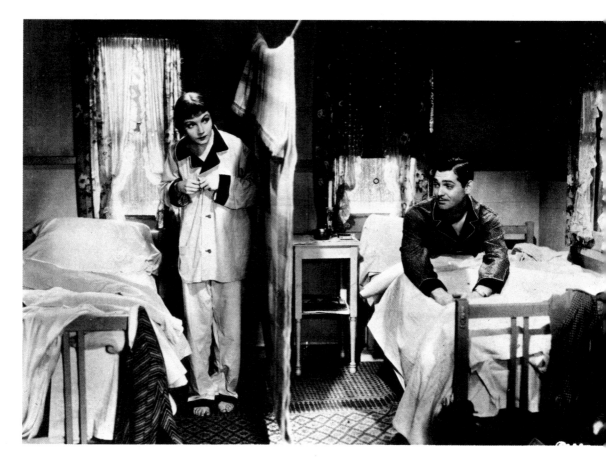

summate grace, and their dances seemed to grow naturally out of the plot, rather than being imposed upon it. To memorable songs by Gershwin, Berlin, Kern, and Porter, they sang and danced with un-equaled charm and exuberance. Their best film was probably 1935's *Top Hat*, directed by Mark Sandrich and choreographed by Astaire. Like most such plots, the story was amiable foolishness. Rogers falls in love with Astaire, only to discover that he is the husband of an old friend of hers. He isn't, of course, but it takes the whole film for her to find that out. There is an aura of freshness and ingenuousness throughout the picture, and the dancing is sublime, beginning with the opening number in which Astaire, dancing in his hotel room late one night, wakes up the lovely lady in the room below. After she complains in person—and he falls in love with her—he sprinkles sand from an ash-tray onto the floor over her head and softly and lovingly dances her to sleep. Later, he dances on the roof of a hansom cab she's riding in—and, in a park pavilion during a rainstorm, they dance their way into love. Arlene Croce writes in *The Fred Astaire and Ginger Rogers Book*:

> Basically, this duet is a challenge dance (he does a step, she copies it, he does another, she tops it, and so on) ... but there is nothing common about the way these dances are executed, and their freshness has noth-ing to do with the lexicon of tap technique. ... In the duet with Rogers ... the point isn't tap-dancing, it's romance. And in "Lovely Day" every step has the dewiness of fresh, young emotion. Those spurting little phrases that end in a mutual freeze (when the music stops, starts

and stops again on uneven counts) as if to say "try and catch me," and that ecstatic embrace, when they pivot together in a wide circle all around the stage, whipping it into a froth—if this isn't perfect dancing, it is the perfect joy that dancing like this aims for and a shining moment in the history of the musical film.

Audiences came to think of Astaire and Rogers as an entity, and they were disappointed when the performers went their separate ways at the end of the decade. Equally popular as a team, albeit a nondancing one, were debonair William Powell and pug-nosed Myrna Loy, who starred in MGM's 1934 film *The Thin Man* and startled moviegoers by playing a happy couple who find marriage an enjoyable state. As Nick and Nora Charles in a series of pictures, Powell and Loy drank a great deal, wisecracked a lot, kissed often, and had a good time together.

The chemistry was also right between Clark Gable and Claudette Colbert in *It Happened One Night*, the first in a cycle of "screwball

Busby Berkeley, the master of the mindless extravaganza, gave Depression-era audiences a surfeit of cleverly choreographed precision dancing. His films were built around wildly elaborate production numbers featuring such whimsical devices as high-stepping pianos and human harps (right). To escape the vacuity of Berkeley's world and the fetters of the Production Code, Hollywood in the 1930's invented an entirely new genre, the screwball comedy. The first— and in many ways the best—of these light, witty, improbable farces was It Happened One Night, *directed by Frank Capra and starring Clark Gable and Claudette Colbert (left above).*

comedies." Written by Robert Riskin and directed by Frank Capra in 1934, *It Happened One Night* was a low-budget sleeper that had been regarded as a comedown for both stars. Instead it won every award available and earned a fortune for Columbia Pictures. Colbert, a heiress running away from her father because he won't approve of her marriage to a glamorous ne'er-do-well, and Gable, an unemployed newspaperman, find themselves sharing a seat on a cross-country bus. Gable recognizes both the girl and his chance for a lucrative scoop and befriends her. Naturally they fall in love despite their initial animosity. All misunderstandings are overcome, and at film's end Colbert elopes with Gable. The charm of the stars, the skill of Capra's direction, and sprightly dialogue made the film a joy. In one scene Gable, unable to thumb a ride, gives up in disgust, only to have Colbert show him how to do it. She displays her leg to an oncoming motorist, who screeches to a halt. One running gag concerns a blanket hanging from a clothes line that separates the beds of the two stars when they share a motel room for economy's sake. Dubbed the "Walls of Jericho," the blanket comes tumbling down when Gable blows a trumpet at the film's end.

Although distinguished by sophisticated, bright dialogue, fast action, and lots of sight gags, screwball comedies also depended on the appeal and comic skill of their stars. Fortunately, Hollywood did not lack for stylish performers in the 1930's, and as a result these comedies still seem fresh and entertaining. Among the most memorable examples of the genre are: *My Man Godfrey*, in which madcap heiress Carole Lombard picks up William Powell in a Hooverville during a society treasure hunt and makes him the family butler; *Bringing Up Baby*, in which Katharine Hepburn and Cary Grant deal with dinosaur bones and a pet leopard; *The Awful Truth*, in which Irene Dunne breaks up ex-husband Cary Grant's new romance by posing as his vulgar, gum-chewing sister; and *Nothing Sacred*, with Lombard as an heiress who wrongly thinks that she is dying of a rare disease and Fredric March as the reporter who sets out to make a fortune by publicizing her as a national heroine.

After *It Happened One Night*, Capra went on to make one success after another, revealing himself in the process as a populist who believed in rural virtues and individualism. In *Mr. Deeds Goes to Town*, Gary Cooper plays a small-towner who inherits twenty million dollars and moves to the big city, where he is besieged by opportunists and con men as well as by pretty Jean Arthur, who makes him a laughing-stock by describing him in her stories as "the Cinderella man." When Deeds decides to give his money away to farmers hard hit by the Depression, he's haled into court by greedy relatives who accuse him of insanity. Naturally Jean Arthur's love and his own convictions give Cooper the strength he needs to defend himself eloquently.

Capra's best picture may well be *Mr. Smith Goes to Washington*, a 1939 release that featured lanky James Stewart as Jefferson Smith, a small-town hero who is appointed to finish the term of a deceased senator. Full of ideals and dreams, Smith resists all attempts to make him a rubber stamp and winds up in open warfare with his former hero, an allegedly distinguished legislator who is really in the pay of corrupt forces. Accused by his opponents of graft, Smith embarks on a filibus-

At its 1934 awards ceremony, the Academy of Motion Picture Arts and Sciences bestowed Oscars on both Gable and Colbert for their performances in It Happened One Night. *The picture itself won an Oscar, and so did Frank Capra, who went on to become the decade's most successful director. Among Capra's notable films was* Mr. Smith Goes to Washington (below), *which pitted James Stewart, a youthful idealist, against his onetime idol, Claude Rains.* Mr. Deeds Goes to Town, *based on the same formula, starred Gary Cooper, who is shown at right, below, relaxing with Capra on the set.*

ter on the senate floor in which he defends himself, reveals the dishonesty he has discovered, and movingly defends the American way.

At a time when Americans wanted to believe that the individual still mattered and that the average man could still control his own destiny, Capra's films found receptive audiences. So too, on a different level, did the Marx Brothers, a lunatic trio who starred in a dozen hilarious films. Groucho, with his greasepaint mustache, omnipresent cigar, slouching walk, peripatetic eyebrows, and constant barrage of wisecracks and insults, was the ringleader. Chico, who dressed like an Italian organ-grinder and affected a heavy accent, was Groucho's shameless cohort; and Harpo—bewigged, angelic-looking, mute—was absolutely unpredictable, as likely to eat a powder puff as rip off the skirt of a passing beauty. In films such as *A Day at the Races* and *A Night at the Opera*, the brothers turned formal, decorous environments into total chaos. In the latter film, for instance, the climax takes place at the Metropolitan Opera during a performance of *Il Trovatore*. Groucho hawks peanuts and popcorn in the auditorium while the other two, dressed as extras, cavort onstage, wave to the audience, and scale the scenery.

W. C. Fields worked alone, but he was every bit as funny as the Marxes. A former juggler and vaudeville star, he became the screen's foremost misanthrope—"Any man who really hates small children and animals can't be all bad," he said in one film. Fields, whose trademarks

The coming of sound added a new dimension to screen comedy without diminishing the importance of the time-tested techniques of the silent era. Indeed, Harpo Marx—who starred with brothers Groucho, Chico, and Zeppo in a succession of zany slapstick comedies in the 1930's and 1940's (left)—remained mute throughout, relying exclusively on mime to delight audiences. W. C. Fields (above right), the era's greatest comic, is best remembered for his vinous ill-humor and his idiosyncratic delivery, but he was also a masterful juggler and a superb sleight-of-hand artist.

were his bulbous nose and straw hat, played "straight man to a malevolent universe which had singled him out for siege and destruction," according to English critic Kenneth Tynan. "He regarded the conspiracy of fate through a pair of frosty little blue eyes, an arm flung up to ward off an imminent blow, and his shoulders instinctively hunched in self-protection. . . . He both looked and sounded like a cement-mixer. He would screw up his lips to one side and purse his eyes before committing himself to speech; and then he would roll vowels around his palate as if it was a sieve with which he was prospecting for nuggets. The noise that finally emerged was something quietly raucous, like the crowing of a very lazy cock. . . . Fields' voice, nasal, tinny, and massively bored, is that of a prisoner who has been uselessly affirming his innocence at the same court for centuries; when in *It's a Gift*, he drives a carload of people straight into a large reproduction of the Venus de Milo, his response as he surveys the fragments is unhesitating. 'Ran right in front of the car,' he murmurs, a little wearily."

Chaplin, as has been noted, eschewed sound films throughout the thirties. No one really cared, since the artistic level of his work remained as high as ever. Indeed many regarded his 1931 release, *City Lights*, as his best film; certainly it is his most poignant. It recounts Chaplin's love for a blind flower girl who mistakenly believes that he is a rich man. Chaplin steals a large sum of money, pays for an operation to restore her vision, is ultimately apprehended, and is sent off to jail. Years later, the girl sees a tramp passing by. Amused at his comic appearance and saddened by his plight—he is being chased by a gang of mocking boys—she goes outside to give him a coin and a flower. When she touches his hand, she realizes that he is her former benefactor. "You?" she asks, stunned by the realization that the handsome lover she had envisioned is really a comical tramp. Her distress and disappoint-

ment, his joy and shame—combined with an awareness that their relationship cannot last—provide an unforgettable end to an enormously moving film. No Chaplin film lacks comic moments, however, and *City Lights* is no exception. Who can forget the society party at which Charlie accidentally swallows a whistle and then, during an attack of the hiccups, produces a crescendo of whistling that disrupts a concert, attracts a pack of dogs, and summons unwanted taxicabs?

Thornton Wilder remarked in the late 1920's that the cinema's only authentic geniuses were Chaplin and Walt Disney. During the pre-World War II era, Disney, the most famous of all screen animators, was the darling of the critics. His Silly Symphonies and Mickey Mouse shorts poked fun at the pretentious and the unjust, and Mickey, who opposed violence but would fight for what he thought was right, struck audiences as the perfect Depression hero. Disney's inventive use of color and sound, inspired slapstick comedy, and ingratiating characters made his films popular all over the world. Toward the end of the decade, he began turning out feature-length animated films—the first was *Snow White and the Seven Dwarfs*—that were enormously successful but that impressed the critics as being less fresh and appealing than his earlier work. By the time of his death, Disney headed a gigantic empire that included television programs, amusement parks, and a profitable procession of uninspired live-action films that were a far cry from the inventiveness of his early work.

If the critics eventually soured on Disney, they never lost their admiration for Garbo, who retains her allure thirty years after her self-imposed retirement. At least partly on account of the skill of MGM's lighting experts, cameramen, and makeup artists, Garbo achieved near-legendary status during the 1930's. Among her sound films were *Grand Hotel*, an all-star epic in which she plays a world-weary ballerina in love with jewel thief John Barrymore; *Camille*, George Cukor's version of Alexander Dumas's story about a beautiful courtesan who gives up the young man she loves at his father's behest; and Ernst Lubitsch's *Ninotchka*, in which she plays her first real comedy role, that of a dedicated Communist who is sent to Paris on business and falls in love with a useless but handsome Westerner. "What, when drunk, one sees in other women, one sees in Garbo sober," writes Kenneth Tynan, one of her countless admirers.

Bette Davis, whose talent and nervous energy lighted up the screen, is another contender for the title of leading lady of the cinema. She reached stardom in 1934 as Mildred in the film version of Somerset Maugham's *Of Human Bondage*. Playing the heartless waitress who takes cruel advantage of Leslie Howard's love for her, she gave what *Life* magazine described at the time as "probably the best performance ever recorded on screen by a U.S. actress." Although she became the undisputed queen of Warner Brothers, she was forced to fight constantly for good roles, and she was often obliged to squander her unequaled ability to play neurotic heroines on distinctly inferior parts. The best of her 1930's films were *Dark Victory*, in which she plays a socialite who succumbs to a fatal disease, and *Jezebel*, in which she is a willful Southern belle who, to her eventual distress, flaunts all conventions.

At MGM, which boasted "more stars than there are in heaven," Norma Shearer, the wife of production head Irving Thalberg, got her pick of roles, which included confession dramas like *The Divorcee* and prestigious adaptations such as *The Barretts of Wimpole Street* and *Romeo and Juliet*. An appealing performer, Shearer had both sex appeal

The thirties witnessed the rise of dozens of new stars, among them such enduring talents as Bette Davis and Henry Fonda, seen opposite in Jezebel, *a 1938 film that brought Davis her second Oscar. Spencer Tracy— at left below with the ill-fated blond Venus, Jean Harlow—also won an Oscar in 1938, his second in succession. Another intriguing aspect of thirties cinema was the degree to which it accommodated old vaudevillians who were not actors in the accepted sense. The best loved of these was Will Rogers (right below), whose personality generally triumphed over the roles he was assigned.*

and elegance. Needless to say, the latter word was never applied to Shearer's contemporary, Jean Harlow, the famous "platinum blond." Her appeal to men was frank and blatant, but she was also a capable comedienne, as she revealed in such films as *Dinner at Eight* and *Red Dust*. Harlow was only twenty-six when she died of uremic poisoning in 1937, and her death shocked the moviegoing public just as Marie Dressler's death from cancer had three years earlier. After a long, checkered career in show business, Dressler had unexpectedly become MGM's highest paid star when she was in her sixties. Her secret, as one film critic has pointed out, was that when she played a great lady she

The most popular film star of the thirties—and perhaps of all time—was a small mouse named Mickey (left). Walt Disney, the animator who created Mickey and supplied his high-pitched, timorous voice, went on to produce such feature-length cartoons as (clockwise from top): Snow White, Pinocchio, *and* Bambi.

added a touch of tramp, and when she played a tramp she included a touch of great lady.

Joan Crawford, another member of MGM's pantheon, achieved stardom in the thirties and clung to it tenaciously despite the fact that most of her films were undistinguished. A shop-girl's idol, Crawford specialized in playing poor girls from the wrong side of the tracks who achieve great riches by sheer determination. A far different screen image was projected by Katharine Hepburn, a born aristocrat whose portrayal of John Barrymore's daughter in *Bill of Divorcement* (1932) began a film career that was still flourishing more than forty years later. Memorable performances in *Little Women*, *Morning Glory*, and *Alice Adams* won her acclaim. "Here is something new and different," reported the *London Daily Telegraph*, "a very young actress with the power of a well-trained tragedienne, a strange, dynamic and moving young person in a profession full of characterless, synthetic blondes." Curiously enough, by the end of the decade Hollywood's powers-that-be had decided that the beautiful Bryn Mawr graduate, with her high cheekbones and aloof manner, was finished in films.

Hollywood in the 1930's also produced a large number of genuinely

unique and capable actors whose films were far more interesting than those of such conventionally handsome leading men as Robert Taylor, Tyrone Power, and Errol Flynn. In films ranging from *Dr. Jekyll and Mr. Hyde* to the screwball comedy *Nothing Sacred*, Fredric March was a superb actor of unusual range and depth. James Cagney and Edward G. Robinson built long and distinguished careers on their gangster films. Topping the box-office polls throughout the decade were three very unlikely stars: Will Rogers, Wallace Beery, and Mickey Rooney. Rogers, who broke into show business as a laconic, lariat-swinging comic with the Ziegfeld Follies, became a major star in

a series of homespun films like *State Fair* and *David Harum*. Beery, a temperamental actor who specialized in playing gruff but lovable galoots, was at his best when he played opposite Marie Dressler in films like *Min and Bill* and *Tugboat Annie*. Rooney was a refreshing change from the angelic little boys who generally appeared in movies; he played either tough slum kids or normal, small-town American boys like Andy Hardy who feared God and their fathers but managed to get into mischief anyway.

Rooney starred in several films with Spencer Tracy, the masculine, likable Irish-American actor who began his career in gangster films but broke the mold with *Fury* and *San Francisco* in 1936. He received back-to-back Oscars in 1937 and 1938 for his performances as a Portuguese fisherman in Kipling's *Captains Courageous* and as Father Flanagan in *Boys' Town*. Tracy's seemingly effortless but undeniably powerful performances won him the regard of critics and fellow actors alike, leading such contemporaries as Humphrey Bogart to remark, "What is a good actor? Spencer Tracy is a good actor, almost the best. Because you don't see the mechanism working, the wheels turning."

Gary Cooper, the tall, extraordinarily handsome son of a Montana

judge, first attracted attention in silent films but became a star in *The Virginian* in 1929. He progressed from flapper's idol to respected actor in a wide variety of films including romances such as *A Farewell to Arms*, Westerns, adventure epics, and comedies. By 1939 he was America's highest-salaried citizen, earning $482,819. "He's no Walter Hampden or Maurice Evans," director Howard Hawks once said of Cooper. "He hasn't their range, their stagecraft, their technique. But that's less important in pictures than inner sincerity and conviction. The grand thing about Coop is that you believe everything he says or does."

James Stewart—or Jimmy, as everyone called him—was equally sincere, but unlike Cooper he was not suited to war films or exotic adventures. Tall, skinny, and boyish, he was America personified. The characters he played were frequently awkward and shy, but by the end of his films a man of honesty and determination had been revealed behind the bumbling exterior.

Tracy, Stewart, and Cooper rank as genuine superstars. But the undisputed king of Hollywood in the thirties, and indeed until his death in 1960, was Clark Gable. Although he began his career in the theater, Gable eventually made a screen test in which he appeared, for some inexplicable reason, in a Polynesian costume and with a rose behind his ear. The result was a quick rejection from studio executives, who thought his ears were too big. He did get some small parts, however, and his magnetism soon became apparent. When he slapped Norma Shearer in *A Free Soul*, his stardom was assured. Women loved to see the deep-voiced, mustachioed Gable treat his costars roughly and then make tender amends. Men liked him, too, because he was, as *The New York Times* observed when he died, "consistently and stubbornly all Man." A leading star throughout the thirties, he capped a decade of successes with the biggest hit of all, *Gone with the Wind*.

Prior to its publication, Margaret Mitchell's novel about the Civil War South had been purchased for the screen by David O. Selznick for

Gone with the Wind, *Margaret Mitchell's discursive paean to the Old South, was the succès fou of the 1936 publishing season. Millions read it, millions more discussed it, and when David O. Selznick announced that he had acquired the film rights, the question of who would play the lead roles became a national obsession. Selznick rapidly settled on Gable to play the male lead, but he rejected hundreds of aspirants before selecting Vivien Leigh, a little-known English actress, to play Scarlett O'Hara, the novel's tempestuous heroine. With Olivia de Havilland and Leslie Howard (left) cast in the key supporting roles, shooting began in earnest. The final product, which alternated between intimate love scenes (right) and panoramic crowd scenes (center), was without question the most popular movie of all time.*

a mere fifty thousand dollars. The book became a best seller, and the question of who would play the leads in the movie version assumed the dimensions of a national guessing game. After a protracted search, an exquisite, green-eyed British actress named Vivien Leigh was awarded the role of Scarlet O'Hara, the film's determined heroine. About Rhett Butler, the dashing Northern privateer, there was never any question. The public made it clear that only Gable would be acceptable. To get him, Selznick had to give MGM a percentage of the profits and allow that studio to serve as the film's distributor. MGM made millions as a result, and Gable played the role to perfection. In one famous scene he kicks in the bedroom door to get at Scarlett, his wife. She wakes up the next morning with an enormous smile of satisfaction on her face, and no member of the audience was at all surprised. The final scene, in which Gable walks out on the willful Scarlett with the words, "Frankly, my dear, I don't give a damn" is engrained in every moviegoer's memory.

Today *Gone with the Wind*, which cost almost four million to film, seems marred by its excessive length—three and three-quarter hours—its basically foolish plot, and its racial stereotypes. But it remains good entertainment, thanks primarily to Gable and Leigh. The most profitable of all American films until *The Sound of Music* and *The Godfather* supplanted it, *Gone with the Wind* was a critical and financial success of huge proportions, ending the decade on a note of triumph for Hollywood.

7

Challenge and Response

WHILE HOLLYWOOD FLOURISHED in the 1930's, totalitarianism began to spread across Europe, snuffing out creative film-making as it snuffed out other manifestations of artistic and intellectual freedom. In Germany, there was a final flowering of the cinema before the Nazi takeover in 1933. In addition to Von Sternberg's *The Blue Angel*, a number of other German films won international esteem. Three of them were the work of G. W. Pabst: *Westfront 1918*, a sentimental but effective anti-war film; *The Threepenny Opera*, a trenchant adaptation of the Brecht-Weill musical about London lowlife; and *Comradeship*, in which French and German miners forget national differences when an accident occurs in a mine on the border between the two countries. *Mädchen in Uniform*, directed by Leontine Sagan, provided German audiences with a chilling view of life in a girls' boarding school run by a militaristic Prussian. And Fritz Lang's 1931 masterpiece, *M*, offered Peter Lorre's memorable portrayal of a child-murderer who is hunted down simultaneously by the police and by the underworld, which is revolted by the nature of his crimes and disturbed by the resultant increase in police activity. The criminals catch Lorre first and subject him to trial by kangaroo court in a tense climax to a psychological thriller of enormous impact.

When Hitler and his henchmen came to power, it quickly became evident that films preaching peace and brotherhood, like those attacking militarism and nationalism, would no longer be tolerated. Lang was just one of countless German film-makers, many of them Jewish, who fled the country. Under Propaganda Minister Joseph Goebbels, German films of the Nazi era were restricted to espousals of party propaganda, preaching hatred of the enemies of the Third Reich or offering bland escapist entertainment. Only in the field of documentary films was Nazi cinema distinguished. Leni Riefenstahl, a former actress, directed *Triumph of the Will*, a record of the 1934 Nazi Party conference at Nürnberg, and *Olympia*, a film about the 1936 Olympics in Berlin, both of which were hymns to the Nazi philosophy. Today their great artistry is recognized, although the circumstances of their creation are impossible to forget.

In Communist Russia, firmly under Stalin's control, "social realism" was the goal of government officials who believed that films of intellectual sophistication or artistic innovation were somehow antiproletariat and that only straightforward, realistic pictures could entertain and

instruct the Russian people. As a result, the Soviets produced dozens of mundane films honoring various heroes of the Revolution. Later in the decade, movies about figures from Russia's more distant past became acceptable, and it was thus that Sergei Eisenstein, greatest of all Soviet film-makers, was given the opportunity to make *Alexander Nevsky*.

Accused of "formalism" by the state, Eisenstein had not completed a film in ten years. But his unique talent was evident again in *Alexander Nevsky*, a sweeping spectacle about a thirteenth-century hero, Prince Alexander, who defends Russia from an invasion by Germanic knights. The film's centerpiece is a battle on the ice of the Neva River during which the Russians defeat the helmeted Germans in fierce hand-to-hand combat.

Foremost among the new Russian talents at work in the thirties was Mark Donskoi, creator of a lovely Gorky trilogy—*The Childhood of Gorky*, *My Apprenticeship*, and *My Universities*—all based on Maxim Gorky's autobiographical writings. Filmed between 1938 and 1940, these three films capture the vitality and humanity of life in the Russian provinces as few other movies have ever done.

After war broke out in Europe, the documentary film flourished in Russia as elsewhere in Europe. Superb battlefield coverage marked film after film, but none surpassed Dovzhenko's *Battle for the Ukraine*, released in 1943. David Robinson has pointed out that the material was actually photographed at various points along the front by two dozen different cameramen, but Dovzhenko "is said to have given each of them detailed advance instructions, and even drawings of what he wanted. In the finished film the images sweep along with the inevitability of a musical structure."

Russia's film studios were moved eastward when Germany invaded

Appropriately enough, it was Joseph Stalin, archtyrant of twentieth-century Russia, who commissioned Ivan the Terrible, Sergei Eisenstein's epic portrait of the sixteenth-century Russian czar. Stalin conceived of the work as a means of lending historical legitimacy to his iron rule, but what Eisenstein created was a searing psychological portrait of a lonely, paranoid old man driven mad by hatred and self-doubt. The film itself was a work of indisputable genius, its every frame a combination of the architectonic and the purely theatrical (top left). Eisenstein, who poses at top right with members of the cast, was lauded in the West for Ivan, but inside Russia his controversial film was suppressed for a decade and released only after both dictator and film-maker had died. Kozintsev and Trauberg, Eisenstein's talented contemporaries, are best remembered today for their film about a fictional revolutionary, The Youth of Maxim (right).

Stalin's domain in 1941, and it was therefore deep in Central Asia that Eisenstein began work on his last film, *Ivan the Terrible*, *Parts I and II*. Reportedly filmed at Stalin's personal suggestion, Part I glorified the sixteenth-century prince who overcame the power of Russia's feudal lords and the treachery of his own friends and family to forge the Russian nation. Although Ivan resorted to cruel and often repugnant means to achieve his goals, the end results, at least in Eisenstein's eyes, made the means acceptable.

Condemned by some critics as unbearably slow and ponderous, Part I of *Ivan the Terrible* is regarded by others as a towering work of genius. It is easy to understand why Stalin, one of the most ruthless of leaders, approved the first half of the epic; it is equally easy to see why Part II, completed in 1946, was banned by an irate government. Far less effective than Part I, it shows Peter becoming increasingly insane, overwhelmed by hate, bitterness, and doubt as to the legitimacy of his mission. Eisenstein suffered a heart attack on the day he completed editing the film, and he died in 1948. For a decade thereafter his completed masterwork remained under official proscription; it received its first screening in 1958, five years after Stalin's death.

Unlike their German and Russian counterparts, French film-makers of the thirties were not subject to oppressive government control. The expensive conversion to sound, coupled with a worldwide economic depression, resulted in hard times for the major French studios, but independent directors and producers thrived in an atmosphere that was receptive to innovation. René Clair, whose *Sous les Toits de Paris* had opened the sound era so promisingly, followed that success with *Le Million*, an inspired piece of musical nonsense about a winning lottery

The land of Pathé, Méliès, and the brothers Lumière remained a center of artistic experimentation and technical innovation well into the 1930's. It is, for example, director René Clair who successfully integrated plot, dialogue, and song in A Nous la Liberté, his 1932 masterpiece. And it is another Frenchman, Jean Renoir, who produced the definitive study of "the mystery of why men submit to war," Grand Illusion. Erich von Stroheim (below) plays a key role in this haunting film, which also features Jean Gabin, whose long career has spanned many movies and many types of roles (left).

ticket that passes among several characters. *A Nous la Liberté*, released in 1931, was even better. That joyful satire deals with the modern phenomenon of automation, pointing out that the mechanized world is as much a prison for man's spirit as any jail.

Another of the decade's major French talents was Jean Vigo, whose death at the age of twenty-nine in 1934 was an immeasurable loss to world cinema. His *Zéro de Conduite* was a strange, almost surrealistic fantasy about a revolt in a boys' school. Vigo told his story through the eyes of his young protagonists. The principal, for instance, is played by a pompous midget in formal dress, and other adults are represented by straw dummies. Other important French films of the decade included *Poil de Carotte*, Julien Duvivier's moving story about the unhappy youth of an illegitimate boy; Jacques Feyder's witty *Carnival in Flanders*, a costume comedy about the triumph of a group of clever Flemings over their Spanish conquerors in the twelfth century; and Duvivier's *Un Carnet de Bal*, a lovely film about a woman who seeks out all the men who signed her card at a dance many years before. The great comedian Raimu starred memorably in Marcel Pagnol's trilogy of life on the Marseilles waterfront, *Marius*, *Fanny*, and *César*.

Towering over all other French film-makers in this rich period was Jean Renoir, son of the famous Impressionist painter, Pierre Auguste Renoir. His two masterpieces, *Grand Illusion* (1937) and *The Rules of the Game* (1939), are regarded as the finest accomplishments of the French cinema. In the former, Renoir makes an eloquent statement about the absurdity of war and the illusions that allow wars to occur: the illusions that arbitrary national boundaries divide men, that patriotism obliges one man to kill another, and that war is glorious and inspires men to great accomplishments. This most powerful of all anti-war films deals not with battlefront action but with prisoners of war who believe that it is their duty to escape and rejoin the fight.

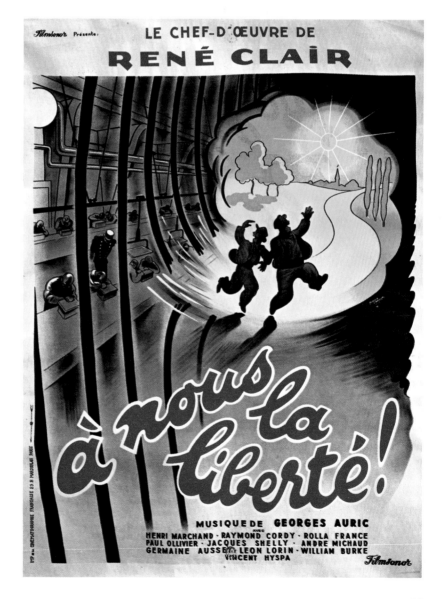

Among the Frenchmen captured by the Germans and interred in a fortresslike villa are three officers: Boeldieu, an elegant aristocrat; Maréchal, a self-made man; and Rosenthal, a Jew. The prison's commandant is Von Rauffenstein, an old-school Prussian officer and a former aviator whose injuries have left him unfit for combat. (It was Erich von Stroheim, the great but unemployable director, who created the role of Von Rauffenstein, and it was he who suggested to Renoir that the character wear a metal chin brace and iron corset.) Because Boeldieu is an aristocrat, he is regarded as an equal by Von Rauffenstein, who is sure that he will not betray his trust by attempting to escape. Preying on this sense of trust, the Frenchman arranges a diversion so that his two compatriots can escape, and then, in an unforgettable scene on the villa's parapets, he is hunted down by spotlights and shot to death by Von Rauffenstein. Maréchal and Rosenthal make good their escape and trek across the German countryside together, overcoming their basic differences in a display of cooperative brotherhood. They take refuge at last in a German farmhouse, where a widow gives them shelter and eventually falls in love with Maréchal, pointing up again the absurdity of national enmities. But their ingrained illusions are stronger than love, and the two Frenchmen feel obliged to leave the farm and attempt to cross the border into Switzerland. As they flounder across the snowy countryside toward the boundary line, they are spotted by German soldiers who raise their rifles to fire but realize at the last moment that Maréchal and Rosenthal have crossed the border and are therefore beyond their reach.

The Rules of the Game, Renoir's other masterpiece, was butchered by its distributors, despised by its first audiences, and eventually banned by the Germans during their occupation of France. It was not seen in its original form until the 1950's, when it was recognized at last as a work of great value. Here, in a mood far different from the one evoked by *Grand Illusion*, Renoir satirizes the aimless, immoral society of prewar France, which regarded honor, honesty, and commitment as worthless and accepted all pleasures as permissible so long as a certain degree of discretion was observed. Set in and around a great château, the film deals with the resident nobleman, his flirtatious wife, the heroic transatlantic flyer who loves her, and a variety of guests and servants—in short, a microcosm of corrupt contemporary society. *The Rules of the Game* is not a likable film because its characters are so reprehensible, but Renoir's artistry makes it an unforgettable experience.

Renoir, Clair, Feyder, Duvivier, and a number of other leading directors left France prior to the Nazi takeover in 1940. Under the censorship imposed by the Nazis in the north and the Vichy government in the south, films of meaning and depth were impossible, and those film-makers who remained turned to escapist fare and to costume dramas that evoked the past, attempting to blot out the awful present.

The most famous of these wartime films is Marcel Carné's *Les Enfants du Paradis*, from a script by Jacques Prévert—a lush and romantic lament for a mankind doomed to be swept along by fate and by illusion. Set in nineteenth-century France, it takes place against a theatrical background (*les enfants* of the title are the common people who buy seats in the uppermost galleries of the playhouse) and implies that life is as much an illusion and a deception as staged dramas.

There were few other French films of distinction during the war. In England, on the other hand, the valorous and successful fight to preserve that nation's liberty was reflected by a number of excellent movies. The sound era had begun grimly for England's film-makers, for no country felt Hollywood's supremacy more keenly; audiences clearly preferred American films to the homemade products, and a law demanding that a certain percentage of each distributor's list be comprised of British films resulted only in a spate of so-called "quota quickies," most of which were produced only to meet the letter of the law and were devoid of merit. There were some notable talents at work, however, and they were heartened in 1933 by the tremendous international success of a British film called *The Private Life of Henry VIII*. Produced and directed by Alexander Korda, a Hungarian by birth, the film was built around a bravura performance by Charles Laughton as the gluttonous, much-married sovereign. On the profits from *Henry VIII*, Korda was able to open his own studios, where many foreign directors came to work, among them Clair, Flaherty, and Feyder.

Another important English producer of the period was Michael Balcon. It was he who allowed Flaherty to make his astonishingly stark 1934 documentary, *Man of Aran*, about life on a barren island in the Irish sea. And it was he who presented such talented British players as Will Hay, Gracie Fields, and Jessie Matthews in a series of unpretentious but entertaining musicals and comedies.

It was also Balcon who sponsored the first film by the most talented of all British directors, Alfred Hitchcock. The supreme master of cinematic suspense came to films in 1920 as a title designer. He worked as a

After almost a decade of restless exile, Hungarian director Alexander Korda settled in London in 1933 to direct The Private Life of Henry VIII. *Korda's witty, irreverent film, a showcase for the flashy talents of Charles Laughton (left above), delighted audiences at home and abroad and spurred the growth of English cinema.* Les Enfants du Paradis, *the greatest French film of the war years, is a fiercely Gallic story of chance, illusion, betrayal, and denial. The role of Baptiste, the pantomimist who is the movie's protagonist, is played by the noted mime Jean-Louis Barrault (above).*

101

script editor, art director, and assistant director before Balcon gave him a chance to direct his first film in 1925. The following year he made *The Lodger*, the first in a long series of Hitchcock thrillers that would make his name synonymous with suspense. During the 1930's, Hitchcock turned out some of the most entertaining films ever made, including *The Man Who Knew Too Much*, *The Thirty-Nine Steps*, *Sabotage*, *Secret Agent*, and *The Lady Vanishes*.

Perhaps the quintessential Hitchcock film is *The Thirty-Nine Steps*, made in 1935. It presents a classic Hitchcockian situation, one in which an innocent man suddenly finds himself in a terrifying dilemma. He is wanted simultaneously by the police, for a murder of a young woman he had befriended, and by the agents of an international espionage ring because the woman, a government agent, has told him about their activities. All the Hitchcock trademarks are present: suspense (will the hero find the head of the spy ring—an unknown villain with a missing finger —before he is himself apprehended?); romance (at one point the hero, Robert Donat, finds himself handcuffed to Madeline Carroll, one of those beautiful, cool blonds who appear so often in Hitchcock films); irony (the archfiend is a respectable British squire who entertains the local clergy on Sundays); humor (rushing into a Salvation Army meeting while eluding the police, the hero is mistaken for the awaited speaker and is forced to improvise an address); violence (a music-hall mentalist, the spy ring's conduit for smuggling military secrets, is shot during his act); and constant cinematic inventiveness.

Lured by the incomparable technical facilities of the Hollywood studios, Hitchcock left England in 1939; his departure was an enormous blow to the British film industry. There were other talented directors at work, however, notably Anthony Asquith, son of a former prime minister. His major films included *A Cottage on Dartmoor*, a tragic love story; *Tell England*, in which the World War I landings at Gallipoli are reenacted; and a brilliant *Pygmalion*, which Asquith's direction and the marvelous acting of Leslie Howard and Wendy Hiller made the best screen adaptation of a play by Shaw.

Simultaneously a group of extremely talented directors was working under John Grierson in the field of documentary films. Produced under the aegis of various government agencies and later under the sponsorship of private industry, these remarkable documentaries recorded with great artistry many aspects of British life. Grierson was the pioneer—his *Drifters*, made in 1929, dealt with the herring fishermen of the North Sea—and his disciples were numerous. Among the notable documentaries were Basil Wright's lyrical *Song of Ceylon* (1934) and Wright and Harry Watt's *Night Mail* (1936), which followed the night run of one particular mail train across England and used poetry by W. H. Auden and music by Benjamin Britten.

The outbreak of World War II, with its brutal air raids on the civilian population of the British Isles, was marked in England by the closing of the cinemas. They were soon reopened, however, and seen on their screens was a remarkable array of British films in which both the commercial film-makers and the documentary directors paid tribute to and helped propagate the national pride and stamina that buoyed the British war effort. Among these documentaries, Watt's *Target for Tonight*, about a raid on Germany, showed the British that their misery was being repaid in kind; *Fires Were Started* led a critic to call Humph-

rey Jennings "the only real poet the British cinema has yet produced."

From the commercial studios, too, came effective films about the war, particularly Asquith's *We Dive at Dawn* and Michael Powell's *One of Our Aircraft Is Missing*. None was better, however, than *In Which We Serve*, filmed by Noel Coward and David Lean from a script by Coward, who also played the leading role. Told in flashback, as the men of the torpedoed British destroyer *Torrin* cling to life rafts and wait for rescue, the film relates the history of the ship from its launching to its destruction, focusing on the brave crew and their loyal families and paying tribute to the patriotism and strength of purpose that had already helped Britain survive five years of war.

A different type of hymn to the British spirit was Laurence Olivier's magnificent film version of Shakespeare's *Henry V*, released in 1945. The technical difficulties encountered in filming a lavish costume spectacle during the austerity of wartime were overcome, and the two-million-dollar budget was more than justified by the film's contribution to national morale. The story of a valorous band of Englishmen who defeat a more numerous Continental foe was obviously timely, and Olivier's moving speech to his troops before the battle of Agincourt seemed an exhortation to the war-weary nation as a whole.

There were, of course, many British films that did not deal directly with the war. Among the finest were Carol Reed's *The Stars Look Down*, which focused on the life of British miners; Michael Powell's *The Life and Death of Colonel Blimp*, a panoramic look at modern British history; and three David Lean films from Noel Coward material: *This Happy Breed*, the hilarious *Blithe Spirit* (featuring Margaret

Rutherford's delightful performance as an eccentric medium), and *Brief Encounter*, in which Celia Johnson and Trevor Howard portray two middle-aged people involved in a doomed love affair.

As the tide of war turned decisively against the Nazis, the Italian cinema suddenly came back to life. During Mussolini's long reign, the Fascists had gained control of the industry by offering irresistible financial rewards and patronage to cooperative producers. Few films were openly Fascist in content, but censorship hung heavy over film-makers, and pitifully few films of distinction were produced. But in 1945, after the fall of Mussolini, Roberto Rossellini's *Open City* burst upon the world's screens and changed the history of the cinema. A graphically realistic portrait of the misery of Rome during the German occupation, *Open City* was shot mostly on the streets, often with concealed cameras, and its cast (headed by the magnificent Anna Magnani) con-

Freed of the Fascist yoke, Italian directors began to recapitulate the sorry history of the war years and their aftermath. The veil of violence had only just lifted when documentary film-maker Roberto Rossellini released Open City, *a technically crude yet emotionally wrenching account of the Nazi occupation that starred Anna Magnani (left above), whom many consider the greatest film actress of all time. Two years later Vittorio de Sica directed a virtually untrained cast in* Shoeshine *(right), an exposé of black market corruption in postwar Rome.*

sisted mostly of nonprofessionals. The film stock used was inferior, and the lighting primitive. Nevertheless, the film was shatteringly effective. It was soon followed by two other classics of so-called "neorealism": Rossellini's *Paisàn*, a story of the closing months of the war in Italy, and Vittorio de Sica's *Shoeshine*, a film about Rome's homeless delinquent children who survived the immediate postwar years by working in the black market.

Not surprisingly, these films, marvelous though they were, did not appeal to Italian filmgoers, who were still living through the dreadful period the films portrayed. For audiences elsewhere, however, they were a revelation. Their realism and passionate conviction made the typical Hollywood film seem artificial and superficial. A new era of film-making was clearly at hand.

8

Hollywood's Fading Glory

"THE LIGHTS ARE GOING OUT in Europe! Ring yourself around with steel, America." That warning, fervently delivered by Joel McCrea at the end of Hitchcock's espionage drama *Foreign Correspondent* in 1940, was but one of Hollywood's many denunciations of Fascism in the years prior to America's entry into the war. Movies such as *Confessions of a Nazi Spy* and *The Mortal Storm* dealt with the Nazi menace head on, while others approached the same topic from a more oblique angle. Howard Hawks's fine film *Sergeant York*, for example, underlined the perils of the present with an episode from the past. With Gary Cooper giving a strong performance as a pacifist who becomes a World War I hero, the movie delivered a clear message to isolationists who felt that America was being drawn inexorably into an overseas war. Charles Chaplin, as expected, made his statement through comedy—before the extent of Hitler's genocidal aims became known. In *The Great Dictator* Chaplin portrays a Jewish barber who is an exact double for Hynkel, the mustachioed, anti-Semitic dictator of a country called Tomania. In the film's final reel, the barber manages to take the tyrant's place long enough to make an impassioned radio plea for peace and tolerance.

For the most part, however, the years just prior to Pearl Harbor saw Hollywood conducting business as usual and producing a surprising number of genuinely entertaining films. In 1940 and 1941, for example, the studio system released *The Philadelphia Story*, with an incandescent Katharine Hepburn as a Main Line socialite torn between suitors Cary Grant and James Stewart; Alfred Hitchcock's *Rebecca*, in which shy young Joan Fontaine struggles to emerge from the malevolent shadow cast by her new husband's dead wife; *The Maltese Falcon*, John Huston's enthralling film version of the Dashiell Hammett detective story; *The Little Foxes*, which featured Bette Davis as the reprehensible Regina Giddens; and Preston Sturges's lovely comedy *The Lady Eve*, with Barbara Stanwyck and Henry Fonda.

Hollywood had long subscribed to the adage "If you want to send a message, call Western Union," and consequently when Darryl Zanuck announced that he intended to produce a film version of John Steinbeck's Depression-era novel, *Grapes of Wrath*, the industry was stunned. They were all the more surprised when the resultant film, directed by John Ford, proved to be one of Hollywood's finest achievements. This story of a family of Oklahoma sharecroppers who

To some, she was Hollywood incarnate—alternately brazen and coy, haunted and hoydenish. To others, she was a tragic changeling whom death deprived of the opportunity to escape from calendar art into comic art. To all, she was Monroe, the supreme symbol of femininity.

leave the oppressive poverty of the Dust Bowl in hope of finding a better life in California was told with all of Ford's considerable artistry, and it featured compelling performances by Jane Darwell as the matriarch of the clan and Henry Fonda as the son who is driven to radicalism by the intolerable conditions that grind his family down.

The next year, 1941, Ford made *How Green Was My Valley*, which dealt with the exploited coal miners of Wales. It won the film colony's Oscars for best movie and best direction, awards that would certainly have seemed its due had not *Citizen Kane*, now generally regarded as the best American film ever produced, been released that same year. Reluctant to offend William Randolph Hearst, the powerful newspaper magnate whose life and longtime friendship with actress Marion Davies had so obviously inspired the film, Hollywood refrained from honoring the extraordinary Orson Welles film. (Louis B. Mayer had gone so far as to offer to buy the film from RKO and destroy it.)

Citizen Kane was a dazzling movie debut for Welles, a twenty-four-year-old enfant terrible whose brilliant work for stage and radio had already made him famous. RKO had given him carte blanche, and with the collaboration of writer Herman Mankiewicz and photographer

Gregg Toland, he had produced a masterpiece. *Citizen Kane* is the story of Charles Foster Kane, a rich young man who decides to build a newspaper empire and in doing so sacrifices his professed high ideals on the altar of yellow journalism. His personal political ambitions are ruined when his extramarital liaison with a young singer becomes public knowledge and his efforts to make her an international opera star bring him nothing but ridicule. Having alienated his friends and wives and lost a good part of his fortune, Kane spends his last years alone in the enormous art-filled palace he has had erected in Florida.

Told primarily in flashbacks, the film begins with Kane's death: after dropping a paperweight that simulates a snowfall when it is turned upside down, the old man whispers a single word, "Rosebud," and dies. Immediately a strident March-of-Time newsreel begins, reviewing the highlights of Kane's career as the camera had recorded them over the years. It is, however, an unsatisfactory record of a man's life, and a group of journalists decide to probe deeper in an attempt to discover the truth about Kane. Perhaps, they speculate, the word "Rosebud" offers a clue. Then ensues a series of interviews with the key people in Kane's life, each of whom relates the man's story as he or she knew it. The portrait that eventually emerges is one of a grasping, vain, selfish, and ambitious man. "He never gave you anything," an old friend recalls bitterly, "he just left you a tip." In the film's final moments, workmen in Kane's palace are seen destroying unwanted junk. One of the items they toss into the furnace is a child's sled; as it burns, the word "Rosebud" can be seen painted on it.

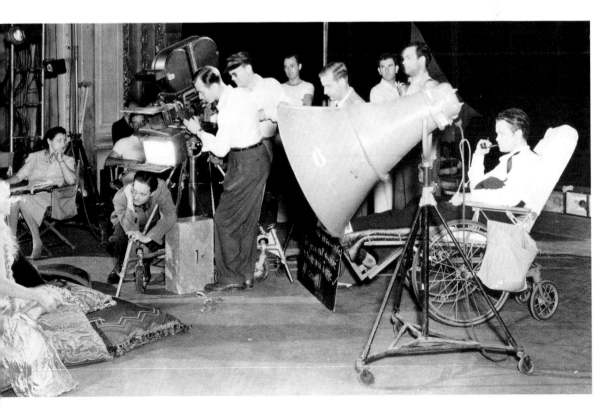

The story of Charles Foster Kane is engrossing but not particularly profound. The movie is a superb piece of film-making, nonetheless, because the techniques employed, although not necessarily new, had never before been used together to such startling effect. Welles and Toland made brilliant use of deep-focus photography and of an arsenal of lighting effects. In the course of the film, flashbulbs pop, spotlights play, the sun's rays pour down into darkened rooms, beams of light are emitted by a movie projector, lightning flashes, and smoke, fog, shadows, rain, and snow all contribute to the almost tangible atmosphere. Quick, dramatic cuts occur throughout. In one famous sequence, Welles employs six fast scenes to portray the disintegration of Kane's first marriage: each shot shows Kane and his wife at the breakfast table, but in each they are clearly more estranged until, in the final shot, they sit in silence as she reads a rival newspaper.

Toland's constantly moving camera is somewhat obtrusive, but it is nevertheless mesmerizing. In the famous sequence at the opera house— the occasion of the second Mrs. Kane's disastrous debut—the camera shows the anguished vocal coach in the conductor's box and then moves upward to the flies, where one stagehand expresses his critical opinion of the performance by holding his nose. Welles's use of sound, ranging from thunder to a cockatoo's screech, reflects his experience in radio.

Citizen Kane was a critical success, but it was not especially profitable, largely because of the reluctance of theater chains to book the film. Orson Welles's next film, *The Magnificent Ambersons*, was cut by RKO against his wishes. Even so, his adaptation of Booth Tarkington's novel about a Midwestern family's fall from riches at the turn of the century bears further testimony to the director's genius. Despite his conspicuous critical success, Welles worked only sporadically after 1942, and he never again reached the cinematic heights attained in his first two films. He remains the premiere hero of many serious moviegoers, however, and *Citizen Kane* is, as French director François Truffaut has remarked, "probably the one [film] that has started the largest number of filmmakers on their careers."

By the time *The Magnificent Ambersons* was released in its truncated form, the United States was at war. Germans and Japanese were depicted as monsters in film after film, and as the war progressed, innumerable movies were made to glorify the American fighting man. Perhaps the best was William Wellman's *The Story of G.I. Joe*, based on the writings of journalist Ernie Pyle. Sympathy for America's beleaguered allies was evoked by such films as William Wyler's *Mrs. Miniver*, in which Greer Garson portrays a noble British housewife bearing up bravely as her fighter-pilot son battles Germans in the skies and her husband helps evacuate troops from Dunkirk. The Roosevelt administration also encouraged Hollywood to build support for the Russians through such films as *Mission to Moscow* and *Song of Russia*.

Far and away the most entertaining of the wartime films is *Casablanca*, which Michael Curtiz directed for Warner Brothers. Humphrey Bogart plays Rick, the expatriate American who runs a successful café in Vichy-controlled North Africa, and Ingrid Bergman portrays one of the refugees pouring into Casablanca in the hope of obtaining visas for

The supreme synthesis of tough talk and spongy sentimentality, Casablanca has assumed a rather special place in the pantheon of great wartime films. Released a few weeks after the Allied landings in North Africa—a happy coincidence for the picture's distributors—Casablanca capitalized on the mystique associated with that campaign. The 1941 film's all-star cast included (left to right below): Claude Rains (in black uniform), Paul Heinreid, Humphrey Bogart, and Swedish actress Ingrid Bergman.

America. *Casablanca* is a marvelously romantic film, filled with such memorable scenes as the one in which refugees and Frenchmen in Rick's café stand and sing "La Marseillaise," drowning out a group of German soldiers who have been bellowing "Deutschland Über Alles."

With few consumer luxuries available, no television to watch, and no gas for cars, Americans went to the movies during the war in record numbers. Their favorite male star of the period was unquestionably Bing Crosby, a former band vocalist whose low-key acting style and pleasant singing voice made him a top box-office draw until the mid-1950's. Whether cavorting with Bob Hope and Dorothy Lamour in a series of wacky "road" films (*Road to Morocco*, *Road to Zanzibar*) or portraying a kindhearted, singing priest in Leo McCarey's *Going My Way*, Crosby was an easygoing performer who wore well. His female counterpart at the head of the box-office polls was the GIs' favorite pinup, vivacious Betty Grable, who, as she herself pointed out, couldn't act, couldn't sing, and could only dance a little. Nevertheless, Grable somehow conveyed the zest, friendliness, and wholesome allure of the all-American girl.

Clark Gable, Spencer Tracy, and Gary Cooper remained preeminent leading men, while Bob Hope—Crosby's wisecracking, ski-nosed side-kick—and the slapstick team of Bud Abbot and Lou Costello were the ranking comedians. Newcomers who became stars during the war years included Van Johnson, the freckled boy-next-door; Alan Ladd, whose portrayals of baby-faced tough guys made female hearts flutter; skinny Frank Sinatra, whose bobby-soxed admirers shrieked and swooned when he sang; and tall, handsome Gregory Peck.

Humphrey Bogart, who had been acting in movies since 1930, could hardly be classed as a newcomer, but despite occasional successes, such as his portrayal of killer Duke Mantee in *The Petrified Forest*, he had failed to emerge an important star. Then came his 1941 performance as Sam Spade in *The Maltese Falcon*, a characterization so compelling that it catapulted him into Hollywood's top ranks, where he remained until his death in 1957. Bogart's indisputable masculinity, his sense of detachment, his cynicism, his bluntness—all were prominent aspects of the screen persona that made him an antiestablishment hero. Among his triumphs were *The Big Sleep*, opposite his wife, sultry Lauren Bacall; *Treasure of the Sierra Madre*; *The African Queen*, with Bogart as a drunken river captain who is inspired by spinster Katharine Hepburn to make an arduous trek down a river to blow up a German gunboat during World War I; and *The Caine Mutiny*. "There isn't an actor in American films today," Pauline Kael wrote ten years after Bogart's death, "with anything like his assurance, his magnetism or his style."

Cary Grant was another performer who attained real stardom relatively late in his career. Initially, Grant's talents were wasted in roles where he was little more than a foil for larger-than-life stars like Mae West, Tallulah Bankhead, and Marlene Dietrich. A string of excellent

comedies in the late 1930's changed all that, and in the forties he came to be regarded as a top box-office attraction. Ranging from sophisticated comedy (*The Philadelphia Story, Mr. Blandings Builds His Dream House*) to Hitchcock melodramas (*Notorious, Suspicion*) and occasional character roles (*None But the Lonely Heart*), he became the epitome of the debonair, charming, and ageless movie hero.

Grant's costar in *Notorious* was Ingrid Bergman, who was billed as "the new Garbo" because of her Swedish birth but who offered a warmth and openness, in contrast to Garbo's mystery, that made her an immediate favorite. Her love scenes with Grant in *Notorious*, remarkable for their length and intensity, capitalized upon Bergman's great beauty; other major roles—in *Casablanca, For Whom the Bell Tolls*, and *Gaslight*—revealed her dramatic talent as well. After the war Bergman became the center of an international scandal when it was discovered that she was to bear Roberto Rossellini's child even though she was still married to another man. Widely denounced for behavior that

Three great directors, three film classics: Notorious *(right), a five-finger exercise from the past master of the suspense thriller, Alfred Hitchcock, that starred two of the era's biggest box-office attractions, Cary Grant and Ingrid Bergman;* The African Queen *(above), impeccably cast and tautly directed by John Huston, who drew an Oscar-winning performance from Bogart and a captivating one from Katharine Hepburn; and* All about Eve, *seen opposite, for which director Joseph L. Mankiewicz won his second consecutive Oscar. Mankiewicz also contributed the film's mordant dialogue, which gave bite to confrontations between the 1950 movie's female leads, Anne Baxter and Bette Davis.*

would become commonplace in the movie business less than a score of years later, Bergman was ostracized from American films until 1957, when she returned to great acclaim in *Anastasia*. Rivaling Bergman for dramatic laurels were MGM's Greer Garson, who specialized in characterizations of noble ladies; Bette Davis, who continued to appear in one entertaining film after another, including *Now, Voyager* and *The Letter*; versatile Barbara Stanwyck, who donned a blond wig to give a smoldering performance in *Double Indemnity;* and Olivia de Havilland, who triumphed in *The Snake Pit* and *The Heiress*. No one ever described Rita Hayworth as a great actress, but the gorgeous redhead made an indelible impression on many moviegoers, none of whom was likely to forget her as she appeared in *Gilda*, wearing a skintight black gown with long black gloves, which she peeled off as she sang "Put the Blame on Mame, Boys."

The first of the postwar years, 1946, was the most profitable in Hollywood history, with audiences flocking to see films as disparate as *The Jolson Story*, a musical biography, and *The Best Years of Our Lives*, a Samuel Goldwyn-William Wyler drama about three returning servicemen and the difficulties they face in readjusting to civilian life. To the casual observer, these were halcyon years for the film industry. Most outsiders—and many movie people—failed to comprehend at the time that the slow but steady decline of the major studios had already begun. First, labor problems struck the industry, resulting in trimmed production budgets. Then came the so-called "red scare," with congressional committees investigating writers, actors, and other studio contractees who were suspected of having ties with the Communist party. Some served prison terms for refusing to implicate friends, and many more found themselves blacklisted for years, unable to work except under pseudonyms.

In 1950, a different kind of blow struck: the courts ruled that studio ownership of theaters was a violation of antitrust laws, which meant that studios could no longer be sure of outlets for their steady stream of films. The beginning of this new era in Hollywood history was marked by the rise of independent producers, many of whom made their films abroad rather than in California, and by a great reduction in the number of movies produced by the major studios. The worst development of all, however, was television. With free entertainment available in their living rooms, Americans in alarming numbers simply stopped going to the movies. At first the studios waged open warfare against the new medium: no stars were permitted to appear on the small screen, and no new films were sold to television. Later, of course, television saved the major studios from bankruptcy by paying huge sums for the rights to hundreds of recently made movies.

The answer to Hollywood's dilemma seemed clear at first: give audiences what they couldn't see on television, namely wide-screen spectaculars. Cinerama, a three-screen, three-projector process, was briefly but vastly popular. Next came 3-D, which required that audiences wear special glasses. It was followed by VistaVision, Todd-AO, and CinemaScope, new wide-screen processes that producers hoped would woo back the movie audience; the latter, first used in 1953, was the one generally adopted by the industry.

But big screen or small, 3-D or not, it was apparent that in the long run audiences would leave their television sets only for good movies. The days of regular, habitual movie attendance were gone forever. Quite clearly, Hollywood needed its men of talent and taste as never before, and fortunately there were still many around. John Ford, for example, produced a series of first-rate Westerns that his many admirers count among the finest ever made. Howard Hawks directed comedies and musicals as well as epic Westerns. Perhaps his best postwar film was *Red River*, in which John Wayne and Montgomery Clift clash in a classic confrontation between men of different generations and ideals.

She never said she could act, but then she rarely had to. Her movies—of which Gilda (above) is perhaps the most famous—were little more than showcases for her ample charms, but the largely male audiences that cheered Rita Hayworth's every picture didn't seem to mind. She was more than a favorite pinup; she was the much-married, scandal-ridden reincarnation of the movie queens of a bygone era.

George Cukor, known as a "woman's director" because of his past successes with actresses like Garbo and Hepburn, had a less identifiable style and philosophy; he simply took the best material he could find and made glossy, consistently delightful films. Under his aegis, Ingrid Bergman, Ronald Colman, and Judy Holliday turned in Oscar-winning performances. Cukor also directed Spencer Tracy in two of his most enjoyable films, *Adam's Rib* (with Hepburn) and *The Actress* (with Jean Simmons)—and he guided Judy Garland through the best performance of her career, a musical version of *A Star Is Born*.

It was George Stevens, another veteran, who directed *Woman of the Year*, in which Spencer Tracy and Katharine Hepburn were first co-starred. This most unlikely of combinations—the pugnacious Irishman—the beautiful Connecticut aristocrat—struck sparks on screen and off. In *Woman of the Year*, Tracy plays a sportswriter and Hepburn an international political pundit who is interested in prime ministers, not pitchers. Needless to say, Tracy cuts her down to his size in this charming comedy, the first of many films they made together over the next twenty-five years. As for Stevens, he followed a series of commendable forties comedies with a procession of highly regarded dramas during the fifties, including *A Place in the Sun*, with Montgomery Clift and Elizabeth Taylor, and the lyrical *Shane*.

Billy Wilder, a refugee from Hitler's Germany, wrote and directed a slew of excellent films marked by his sardonic view of life. On the heels of *Double Indemnity*, a drama of sexual corruption, came *The Lost Weekend*, with Ray Milland as a hopeless dipsomaniac; then *A Foreign Affair*, with Jean Arthur as a naïve, idealistic American congresswoman pitted against amoral Marlene Dietrich in postwar Berlin; and *Sunset Boulevard*, in which Gloria Swanson gave a magnificent performance as Norma Desmond, a silent screen actress who, twenty years after her last film, still believes she lacks only the proper vehicle for a return to the screen. Her relationship with a calculating young writer, played by William Holden, drives her over the edge into madness, and she shoots him in a jealous rage. The film is packed with unforgettable moments: Swanson and Erich von Stroheim, who plays her husband and former director, conducting a funeral procession at night for her pet chimpanzee; Swanson visiting Cecil B. DeMille on a movie set and coming radiantly to life when the electricians turn powerful lights on her face; Swanson, totally mad, being taken away by the police as Von Stroheim tells her that he is about to shoot a scene that calls for her, as Salome, to descend her palace steps. No other film has dealt as powerfully, and as bitterly, with the impermanence of the illusions spun by Hollywood. Later in the 1950's, Wilder turned to cynical comedy, notably *The Apartment* and *Some Like It Hot*; in the latter, Jack Lemmon and Tony Curtis play witnesses to a gangland murder who avoid being rubbed out by donning female clothes and posing as members of an all-girl band led by Marilyn Monroe.

From Alfred Hitchcock came a steady flow of great entertainment, from *Strangers on a Train* to 1960's *Psycho*. One of his best was *North by Northwest*, which featured Cary Grant in two unique sequences. The first occurs when a small plane chases him across a cornfield as the pilot tries to kill him; the second, when Grant climbs down the presidential faces of Mt. Rushmore while eluding the villains.

William Wyler, another consistently successful film-maker, followed up *The Best Years of Our Lives* with hits such as *Roman Holiday* and *The Desperate Hours*. His multimillion-dollar remake of *Ben-Hur*, with Charlton Heston in Ramon Novarro's old role, earned a fortune for MGM in 1959. John Huston's first postwar film was *Treasure of the Sierra Madre*, one of Hollywood's best. Bogart and Walter Huston play prospectors who find a lode in the mountains of Mexico and then fight with each other for possession of the gold. At the end of the film Mexican bandits, to whom the gold means nothing, kill Bogart for his shoes and scatter the gold dust in the wind—a fitting ending to a powerful drama about the vanity of riches.

Another director whose eminence continued into the 1970's was Fred Zinnemann, a versatile artist whose successes included *High Noon*, with Gary Cooper as a sheriff who goes alone to meet the outlaws who have

The career of director George Stevens spans more than four decades. It began in 1929 with a series of forgotten shorts and it extends well into the 1970's. Some milestones along the way: Woman of the Year *(1946), the first pairing of one of the screen's most effective and enduring duos, Tracy and Hepburn (left);* A Place in the Sun *(1951), Elizabeth Taylor's first demanding role and Stevens's first Oscar-winning film (above); and* Shane *(1953), a flawed but moving Western starring Alan Ladd and Brandon de Wilde (right).*

vowed to kill him, and *From Here to Eternity*, a highly entertaining drama of military life.

Joseph L. Mankiewicz, long one of Hollywood's top screenwriters, turned to directing in the late 1940's, creating such delightfully sophisticated films as *A Letter to Three Wives* and *All about Eve*. Mankiewicz's script for the latter was a witty love letter to the Broadway theater as well as an affectionate but shrewd dissection of its denizens. Anne Baxter plays a young actress who sets out cold-bloodedly to insinuate

herself into the life of a great Broadway star, Bette Davis, and then to supplant her. Davis is superb as Margo Channing, the fading star whose temperamental outbursts cloak her fear of advancing age.

The critics usually sneered at the films of Cecil B. DeMille, but he became a greater box-office draw than most of the stars who appeared in his overblown epics, each of which cost a fortune, took several years to make, and set attendance records when released. *Samson and Delilah*, *The Greatest Show on Earth*, a circus drama, and *The Ten Commandments*, a remake of his 1923 film, were all gigantic moneymakers.

The films of Elia Kazan, on the other hand, were usually critical as well as financial successes. Trained in the New York theater, Kazan turned to movies in 1944, directing a string of acclaimed dramas: *A Tree Grows in Brooklyn*, *Gentleman's Agreement* (about American anti-Semitism), *A Streetcar Named Desire* (with Brando repeated his stage portrayal of Stanley Kowalski and Vivien Leigh giving one of the screen's truly great performances as the fragile, foredoomed Blanche DuBois), *East of Eden* with James Dean, and best of all, *On the Waterfront*. In the latter, Brando gives a flawless performance as a

longshoreman who eventually revolts against the corrupt union officials who dominate the New York harbor.

The musical film—like the Western, a uniquely American product—soared to new heights in the forties and fifties. Fox's brash Grable vehicles and the Crosby films at Paramount were pleasant enough, but it was at MGM that the musical really flowered. Under the aegis of Arthur Freed, a former songwriter whom Louis B. Mayer had put in charge of the studio's musical productions, a group of extraordinarily talented directors, choreographers, and performers turned out a series of groundbreaking musicals in which the songs and dances seemed integral to the plot. Inventive, buoyant, filled with zest and creativity, these musicals were cinematic delights.

Vincente Minnelli, a director brought to Hollywood by Freed, launched the new era with *Meet Me in St. Louis* in 1944. A nostalgic recreation of turn-of-the-century America, it was a joyful tribute to a bygone era and it was beautifully performed by a large cast headed by Judy Garland, who sang "The Boy Next Door," belted out "The Trolley Song" with abandon, and performed a charming cakewalk with young Margaret O'Brien. Minnelli was also the director of *The Pirate*, with Garland and Gene Kelly; *An American in Paris*, which ended with a twenty-minute ballet; and *The Band Wagon* with Fred Astaire.

During the same period Gene Kelly and Stanley Donen directed *On the Town* and *Singin' in the Rain*. The latter, an affectionate satire on the Hollywood of the late 1920's, when sound was throwing studios into chaos, may well be the best musical ever made. Kelly plays a film star in love with chorus girl Debbie Reynolds. Their affair is compli-

Few newcomers to Broadway have so charged the stage with their presence as Marlon Brando did in Elia Kazan's 1951 production of A Streetcar Named Desire. Audiences and critics alike were transfixed by the intensity of Brando's performance, and moviegoers were equally enthusiastic about Kazan's film version of the play (left above), which costarred Vivien Leigh. The director's next major project, a graphically realistic film exposé, On the Waterfront (right), brought Oscars to Brando and his costar Eva Marie Saint (above).

118

cated by the fact that Reynolds is providing the screen voice for Kelly's vain and temperamental costar, Linda Lamont (Jean Hagen), who has an incredibly squeaky voice but nevertheless still thinks that neither the movies nor Kelly can survive without her. The film is fast, funny, and exhilarating, and the musical numbers are nothing less than sublime: Kelly singing the title song as he dances down the street in a torential downpour, Kelly and Reynolds dancing to "You Were Meant for Me" on an empty sound stage, and the great "Broadway Ballet," an elaborate production number that pays tribute to the various musical styles of Hollywood's past.

Kelly was one of the important new stars of the postwar period. Others were William Holden, whose clean-cut sex appeal made him a box-office champ in such films as *Executive Suite* and *Stalag 17*; Burt Lancaster, a former circus acrobat who alternated between swashbuckling adventure films and dramas like *Elmer Gantry*; Rock Hudson, a handsome but stolid performer who became Hollywood's most popular romantic hero for a time; and Montgomery Clift, a gifted actor who gave excellent performances in such films as *A Place in the Sun* and *From Here to Eternity*.

Elvis Presley, a rock-and-roll singer who swung his hips on screen for the first time in 1956, was an immediate sensation who retained his popularity for years despite the derision of critics. Dean Martin and Jerry Lewis were the screen's top comic team until they split up; Lewis then went on to create and direct a string of comedies. But it was Jack Lemmon, who made his screen debut in 1953 opposite the brilliant comedienne Judy Holliday in *It Should Happen to You*, who proved to be the perfect hero for the perplexed fifties. He usually appeared as an unassuming, bewildered, average guy with a lecherous streak that was rarely fulfilled. In *Mister Roberts*, *Some Like It Hot*, and *The Apartment*, he proved himself to be the best light comedian since Cary Grant, while serious dramas like *Days of Wine and Roses* showed him to be an actor of depth and sensitivity.

The major new male star of the decade was, without question, Marlo Brando. A product of New York's Actors Studio, he was an iconoclastic but dedicated craftsman who made his debut in *The Men* in 1950 and captured the nation's fancy a year later with his electrifying portrayal of the brutal Stanley Kowalski in *A Streetcar Named Desire*. Over the next several years he displayed dazzling versatility, playing a Mexican bandit in *Viva Zapata!*, a longshoreman in *On the Waterfront*, and Mark Antony in *Julius Caesar*. No actor was ever more acclaimed, but a disastrous succession of vehicles and an increasing reputation for temperament led to a temporary decline in his fortunes in the 1960's.

John Wayne was never called an exciting actor, but "Duke"—the strong, silent cowboy who stood for all that was good and solid about America—is recognized today as the biggest moneymaker in movie history. (By 1967 his films had grossed $400 million.) Wayne had been in movies since 1928 and had made literally hundreds of cheap Westerns and adventure epics before John Ford starred him in *Stagecoach* in 1939. His box-office status climbed throughout the decade, but he did not really break through as a top star until the late 1940's, when he appeared in two Ford Westerns, *Fort Apache* and *She Wore a Yellow Ribbon*, in Hawks's *Red River*, and in the Marine epic *Sands of Iwo Jima*. His name first appeared on the annual list of the top ten box-office attractions in 1949—and it was still there in 1974, a record that no other star has even approached. Regardless of the mediocre quality of most of his films and his limited acting ability, he is the eternal symbol of the rugged individualism that built the American West.

Judy Garland was another performer whose screen presence exceeded the sum of the roles she played. Americans had loved Garland since her childhood, and they were delighted when she blossomed into an attractive young woman of great talent. *Meet Me in St. Louis* and other films made it clear that she was a fresh and appealing adult performer, a capable actress and an excellent comedienne as well as a singer of unique ability. Then came the well-publicized series of nervous breakdowns, incompleted roles, broken marriages, suicide attempts, and periodic comebacks. Her strong performance in 1954's *A Star Is Born* was therefore enormously gratifying to her fans. Employing her mature talents to the fullest, she sang Harold Arlen's "The Man That Got Away" as if it was the story of her life and etched a convincing portrait of an actress who finds professional success but personal heartbreak.

Another child actress who grew up to be a major star was Elizabeth Taylor, the exquisite brunette whose twelve-year-old beauty had captivated audiences when she appeared in *National Velvet* in 1945. By the time she was seventeen, Taylor was playing love scenes with male stars old enough to be her father. Except for *A Place in the Sun*, her films were undistinguished until the late 1950's, when she appeared in a string of successes, including *Giant*, *Cat on a Hot Tin Roof*, and *Suddenly Last Summer*. She was by then already embarked on a string of divorces, illnesses, and affairs that were to make her a prime box-office attraction and a movie star of the old style.

Among the unique leading ladies of the 1950's was Audrey Hepburn, a totally enchanting actress who could be either an endearing gamin or an elegant sophisticate, depending on the script's requirements. As a princess on a spree in *Roman Holiday*, she captured all hearts, and throughout the decade she gave performances that demonstrated her versatility as well as her unfailing charm. She starred in comedies (*Sabrina*, *Love in the Afternoon*), musicals (*Funny Face*, with Fred Astaire), and dramas (*The Nun's Story*)—and triumphed in all of them. Doris Day, a perky blond who had sung with various big bands before coming to Hollywood, starred in a string of pleasant musicals before embarking in the late 1950's on a series of mildly risqué comedies such as *Pillow Talk* that made her the screen's top female attraction. Grace Kelly, a cool patrician, starred in several excellent films, including *Rear Window* and *The Country Girl*, before abdicating stardom to become Her Serene Highness, Princess Grace of Monaco.

No actress is more representative of the fifties than delectable, vulnerable Marilyn Monroe, whose story is well known: an unhappy childhood in foster homes, a struggle to become a star, the achievement of worldwide sex-symbol status, marriages to and divorces from sports hero Joe DiMaggio and playwright Arthur Miller, the yearning to be

Led by headliners like Judy Garland—seen at left in A Star Is Born*—the musical staged a major comeback in the 1950's. Most of these films were pedestrian, a few were ingratiating, and a handful were inspired. One of the very best was* Singing in the Rain *(right above), a spoof rather loosely based on the fate that befell John Gilbert when the movies learned to talk.*

Overleaf: A portfolio of the industry's most durable stars, identified—for those who need help—on page 186.

accepted as a serious actress, and finally her death, probably suicidal, by an overdose of sleeping pills. She has, in the decade since her death, become a true American legend, a symbol of Hollywood's exploitation of those it canonizes. In such films as *Bus Stop* and *The Prince and the Showgirl*, however, she remains a lovely, ripe blond, desperately unsure of herself but exuding irresistible appeal and unmistakable star quality.

Monroe's last film, *The Misfits*, was also the last film appearance of Clark Gable, who died after its completion in 1962. By then the Hollywood over which they had reigned was already well past its prime. The number of films produced each year had shrunk drastically, and most of those that were being filmed were made abroad, leaving the studio sound stages empty and silent. The long list of contract players, once the glory of the studios, had dwindled to a handful. A new era of international film-making had begun, one in which each film was an individual project, not just one more product of a studio assembly line. Hollywood was a shadow of its former self, although as a symbol of the glamour of the movies it remains permanently enshrined, like Gable and Monroe, in the mythology of the twentieth century.

9

The Universal Art

ROSSELLINI . . . DE SICA . . . KUROSAWA . . . Fellini . . . Antonioni . . . Bergman . . . Godard . . . Truffaut. . . . These distinguished film-makers, their names now as familiar to the world's moviegoers as those of many stars, have written an exciting new chapter in screen history since the end of World War II. With the power of the big studios diminished, these new directors retained full artistic control of their films, and the result was a stream of provocative, highly personal movies.

Italian neorealism was the first important movement in the postwar cinema. Ironically, the Italians themselves were not enthusiastic about Rossellini's *Open City*, Luigi Zampa's *To Live in Peace*, or De Sica's *Shoeshine*. Having experienced firsthand the death throes of Fascism, they had little desire to see the era faithfully depicted on the screen. International critics and perceptive moviegoers, on the other hand, immediately recognized the inherent truth and power of the films despite their technical crudities. De Sica's *The Bicycle Thief*, released in 1948, was probably the best. The story of a poor billposter's search for the stolen bicycle that is essential to his job, it is also a tender, sensitive exploration of the man's relationship with his young son and a revealing depiction of a self-absorbed urban society.

Like its neorealistic predecessors, De Sica's film was frowned upon by the government, which felt that it presented a negative picture of Italian life and was damaging to the tourist trade. Far more acceptable —and lucrative—were *Bitter Rice*, with its widely reproduced shots of buxom Silvana Mangano, dripping wet in the rice fields, and *Bread, Love, and Dreams*, a comedy starring Gina Lollobrigida.

Few Americans had even heard of Federico Fellini, and fewer still could identify his cinematic alter ego, Marcello Mastroianni, but by the end of 1960 virtually all of them knew about La Dolce Vita. Fellini's free-form exploration of Roman decadence—the "sweet life" of the idle, indulged rich—introduced a new generation of moviegoers to a new generation of foreign films, stars, and directors.

In the ensuing years Rome became known as Hollywood-on-the-Tiber, as new sound stages were built for a succession of overstuffed spectacles, most of which proved to be artistically undernourished. Fine films like De Sica's *Umberto D*, the poignant story of an old-age pensioner, were ignored while Italians counted the box-office receipts from Technicolor epics that offered flesh instead of finesse. Serious film-makers found the struggle for financing extremely difficult. Nevertheless, a new group of talented directors did emerge in the 1950's. None of these has been more successful than Federico Fellini. He first won international acclaim in 1953 with the release of *I Vitelloni*, a powerful film about postwar youth, but it was *La Strada*, made in 1954, that marked him as one of Italy's truly gifted directors. The story is simple:

In Hollywood, Cecil B. DeMille
was .remaking The Ten Commandments; in Italy, directors
who rejected the whole notion
of big-budget spectaculars were
turning out a succession of mod-
est black and white films that
were to revolutionze movie-
making. Each was a highly personal statement, one that mani-
festly favored acting over action,
direction over production. Two
of the finest examples: Michelangelo Antonioni's L'Avventura,
with Monica Vitti (left), and La
Strada (opposite), in which director Fellini's wife, Giulietta Masina, played opposite Anthony
Quinn.

an innocent, half-witted girl is bought from her mother by a brutal carnival strongman. He abuses her, murders the sympathetic tightrope
walker who befriends her, and eventually abandons her. Years later,
when he learns of her death, he weeps uncontrollably over her fate and
his own loneliness. Magnificently acted by Giulietta Masina and
Anthony Quinn, La Strada is, William Bayer has written, "a film with
an uncanny power to move people to tears. . . . It is a poem about mar-
ginal people living on the fringes of society. It takes place literally, 'on
the road,' in deserted lots, on beaches between highways and seas. Its
message—that everyone needs someone; that loneliness and solitude are
unbearable—is almost simple-minded, yet it is exquisitely expressed."

With La Dolce Vita, released early in 1960, Fellini achieved both
notoriety and enormous financial success. This film about the hedonis-
tic, amoral life of Rome's "beautiful people" is really a series of
startling episodes held together by a character played by Marcello Mastroianni, a gossip columnist who is himself caught up in the aimless,
scandalous "sweet life." From its unforgettable opening image—a statue
of Christ, arms outstretched, suspended from a helicopter that flies low
over modern Rome—La Dolce Vita moves from one shocking sequence
to another. Filled, like all Fellini films, with stunning, bizarre images
and faces and marked by the director's wild comic imagination, the
film was widely condemned as "vulgar, witless, and intellectually bank-
rupt" and lavishly praised as "a cultural and social document, as well as
an exciting entertainment."

Equally controversial, but far less successful commercially, were
the films of Michelangelo Antonioni. A former scriptwriter and critic,
he eschewed conventional plots and chose instead to focus on the anxiety and rootlessness of modern life. Le Amiche and Il Grido won him
passionate admirers, but it was L'Avventura, released in 1960, that first
brought him to the attention of a wider audience. That film deals with
a group of rich Italians on a yachting party who suddenly realize that

one of the group is missing—Anna, the fiancée of one of the men—and who then conduct a long search for her, a search that becomes more and more perfunctory as the ennui and disconnection of the characters deepens. Dismissed as meaningless and stupifyingly boring by some filmgoers, it has been acclaimed as a masterpiece by others. Pauline Kael, the most distinguished of American film critics, was one of *L'Avventura*'s proponents. "Antonioni's camerawork," she wrote, "is an extraordinarily evocative mixture of asceticism, lyricism and a sense of desolation. He is a master of space: he can take bleak landscapes and compose or transform them into visions of elegance and beauty. The people are rich but the atmosphere is cold; it is upper-class neo-realism —the poetry of moral and spiritual poverty. . . ." "*L'Avventura*," she added in another essay, "is a study of the human condition at the higher social and economic levels, a study of adjusted, compromising man— afflicted by short memory, thin remorse, easy betrayal. The characters are passive as if post-analytic, active only in trying to discharge their anxiety—sex is their sole means of contact and communication. Too shallow to be truly lonely, they are people trying to escape their boredom in each other and finding it there. They become reconciled to life only by resignation. . . . It's a barren view of life but it's a view. . . . A terrible calm hangs over everything in the movie; Antonioni's space is a kind of vacuum in which people are aimlessly moving—searchers and lost are all the same, disparate, without goals or joy."

"Fellini forces reality, Visconti dramatizes reality, I try to undrama-

uze," Antonioni has said. Luchino Visconti, son of an aristocratic Milanese family, is often hailed as a precursor of neorealism because of such starkly realistic films as *Ossessione*, made during the war. After *La Terra Trema* (1948), another film in the neorealistic vein, he turned to lavish period dramas. *Rocco and His Brothers*, a 1960 film about a family of Sicilian peasants, was a partial return to neorealism.

In an era that saw performers move easily from one country's film studios to another, Italy provided several international stars. Anna Magnani, the magnificent, fiery lead in *Open City* and dozens of other Italian films, won a Hollywood Oscar for her role in Tennessee Williams's *The Rose Tattoo*. She was, said Jean Renoir, who directed her in *The Golden Coach*, "probably the greatest actress I have ever worked with. She is the complete animal—an animal created for the stage and screen . . . ." Sophia Loren, a voluptuous and appealing performer, entered films as an extra in costume epics, but producer Carlo Ponti, who became her husband, guided her to stardom in Italian films that took advantage of her natural gift for comedy. In De Sica's *Two Women* she gave an extraordinarily effective dramatic performance as a mother who sees her daughter raped by soldiers. She has been at her best since then in earthy comedies like *Marriage—Italian Style* and *Yesterday, Today and*

Vittorio de Sica's inspired choice of Sophia Loren (left) to play the starring role in Two Women, *a harrowing epic of wartime travail, gave the earthy Italian actress a chance to display her formidable dramatic talents, which won her an Oscar in 1962. The rococo film fantasies of French poet, playwright, novelist, and film-maker Jean Cocteau won few awards, but works such as* Orpheus *(top) and* Beauty and the Beast *(above) demonstrated the degree to which poetic sensibilities could be transferred to film.*

Tomorrow. Loren's costar in the last two films was Marcello Mastroianni, the leading Italian male star of the postwar period. *La Dolce Vita* boosted him to stardom, and he consolidated his position in films ranging from Pietro Germi's hilarious *Divorce—Italian Style* to Antonioni's enigmatic *La Notte*.

In neighboring France, a film industry that had been a leader in world cinema until the German occupation quickly recovered its eminence when the war ended. With government assistance, independent producers flourished, leading directors returned from temporary exile, and a new crop of talented artists came to the attention of moviegoers. Jean Cocteau, whose surrealistic *Blood of a Poet* had startled audiences in 1930, returned to movie-making in 1946 with *Beauty and the Beast*, a lavish version of the old fairy tale. A few years later he made what is generally thought to be his best film, the poetic, expressionistic *Orphée* (1950) with Jean Marais as a modern equivalent of the mythological hero who has a special relationship with death.

Max Ophüls, a refugee from Hitler's Germany who had made films in several countries and who was renowned for his fluid camera work, came to France in 1950 to make a new version of *La Ronde*, Schnitzler's play about a series of interlocking amorous relationships. The Ophüls film, impeccably performed by an all-star cast, was a sophisticated, witty triumph that delighted moviegoers. His masterpiece, however, is *Lola Montes*, which was butchered by its distributors when it was first released in 1955 but which has since been restored to its original form. It is, as David Robinson has written, "a rich, kaleidoscopic impression of the career of the great courtesan, enriched with extravagant rococo decoration and Ophüls' unique camera style."

Robert Bresson was another iconoclastic film-maker and cult favorite. His austere, metaphysical films all dealt with characters in spiritual crisis. *The Diary of a Country Priest*, *Pickpocket*, and *The Trial of Joan of Arc* are sparse, almost abstract films in which plot is subordinate to mood and to the countless details that reveal character. Bresson has made very few films, but he is prolific in comparison to Jacques Tati, one of the true geniuses of postwar French cinema. A former music-hall artist, Tati began his film-making career with several short comedies and then, in 1947, made his first feature, *Jour de Fête*, a hilarious film in which he played a bumbling village postman. Six years later he made *Mr. Hulot's Holiday*, a film about a disaster-prone innocent on a seaside vacation, and in 1958 he repeated the characterization in *Mon Oncle*. Tati has been hailed by many critics as a successor to the great silent film comedians.

Less sublime but certainly more profitable were the films of Roger Vadim, whose *And God Created Woman*, released in 1956, made Brigitte Bardot the international sex symbol of the decade. Far more erotic than Vadim's film was Louis Malle's *The Lovers* (1958), in which the luminous Jeanne Moreau plays a bored socialite who enjoys a night of frankly depicted lovemaking at a country estate. Vadim, who was twenty-eight when he made *And God Created Woman*, and Malle, who was just twenty-five when *The Lovers* was released, were the advance guard of a new group of young French directors who were to revitalize the cinema. These newcomers—including Claude Chabrol, Philippe de Broca, Eric Rohmer, Claude Lelouch, and Agnes Varda as well as the triumvirate of François Truffaut, Jean-Luc Godard, and Alain Resnais—were collectively known as *la nouvelle vague*, the new wave of film-makers who loved movies and wanted to devote their lives to making them. Truffaut, Godard, and many of the others had served as critics for the magazine *Cahiers du Cinema*, and they believed passionately that the director was, or should be, responsible for all aspects of a film, that he should be its sole *auteur*.

Truffaut, who claims to have seen two thousand movies by the time he was twenty, makes films that are accessible, warm, and enormously entertaining, unlike those of his more pretentious contemporaries. His first feature, *The 400 Blows*, which was made in 1959, is a largely autobiographical film about a neglected, misunderstood adolescent who drifts into delinquency. But despite its harsh social commentary, the film is suffused with tenderness and humor. *Jules and Jim*, released in 1961, is still regarded as Truffaut's finest. This lovely and lyrical film tells of the unorthodox triangular relationship of two men and the woman they both love. With Jeanne Moreau giving a superb performance as the mercurial and enchanting heroine, *Jules and Jim* proved to be an utterly captivating film, directed with stunning artistry.

Although Jean-Luc Godard shares Truffaut's love of films, his own movies contain none of Truffaut's warmth or joy of life. *Breathless*, the first important new-wave film to reach America, was dedicated by Godard to Monogram Pictures, the Hollywood studio that specialized in cheaply made gangster films. Its hero, played by Jean-Paul Belmondo, is a cop-killing thief who worships Bogart's screen image and feels no guilt or remorse for his crimes. He is eventually betrayed to the police by the American girl who loves him. Both, as Pauline Kael has pointed out, are totally immoral and terribly attractive. Filmed largely with a hand-held camera and filled with jump cuts, it is a fast, unpretentious, and rather chilling movie. As the sixties progressed Godard was to become less and less interested in narrative structure and more and more dedicated to the revolutionary philosophy he espouses.

The third highly acclaimed French director of the late 1950's and early 1960's was Alain Resnais, who began with a series of documentary films. His first feature film was the powerful *Hiroshima Mon Amour*. Built around the love affair of a French woman and a Japanese architect, it interweaves the woman's recollections of her tragic love for a German soldier during World War II with horrifying scenes of the devastation of Hiroshima. The woman's story is not told in chronological sequence but rather in bits and pieces, as the film moves from present to past and back with great fluidity. "*Hiroshima Mon Amour*," William Bayer writes, "is structured like a piece of music, with themes and variations that entwine, and movements paced at different tempos. It is filled with slow traveling shots, dollies forward, pullbacks, and pans. . . . The picture, finally, has an unforced flow which is extraordinary when one analyzes its intricate structure. It is a film of complements: image and sound; past and present; the actual and the remembered; Hiroshima (a city of Neon) and Nevers (a city of gray stone); the personal

Jacques Tati (above) might fairly be called the Chaplin of the talkies, for the handful of films that he has written, directed, and starred in are sublime comic achievements, direct lineal descendants of the works of Chaplin, Lloyd, and Keaton. Tati is a throwback to another generation however, and modern French film-making has been more influenced by men like Roger Vadim, whose And God Created Woman gave international exposure to Jean-Louis Trintignant and Brigitte Bardot (right).

and the cosmic; a man and a woman; concern for the individual and concern for mankind." Resnais's next film, *Last Year at Marienbad*, an extension of this splintering technique, mystified a good many critics and moviegoers. "It is," Richard Schickel said, "a film quite literally out of this world, a film that at last achieves the aesthetician's dream of absolute abstraction in the movies. It is completely purified of any meaning whatsoever. It therefore allows the spectator to achieve absolute purity of boredom."

During this postwar period, France's leading film actors included Jean Gabin, who gradually eschewed his leading-man image and became a kind of French Spencer Tracy, a much-loved character star; Gerard Philipe, the elegant, versatile star of innumerable films; Jean Marais, the extraordinarily handsome hero of Jean Cocteau's films; Fernandel, the perennially popular comedian; and Louis Jouvet, a brilliant actor who specialized in playing cynical, sly characters. The popular balladeer Yves Montand became a film actor of note in Clouzot's *Wages of Fear*, inaugurating a career in pictures that was to flourish into the 1970's. Alain Delon succeeded Marais as the ladies' romantic favorite, while Jean-Paul Belmondo became, with Godard's *Breathless*, a new

superstar and the archetypal hero of the anguished sixties. "[He] is probably the most exciting new presence on the screen since the appearance of Brando," wrote Pauline Kael; "nobody holds the screen this way without enormous reserves of talent. . . ." Among the ladies, Michèle Morgan and Danielle Darrieux were replaced as reigning favorites by Bardot, Simone Signoret (who demonstrated in Jacques Becker's *Casque d'Or* that she had a unique ability to portray sensuous women in love), and Jeanne Moreau, the favorite acress of *la nouvelle vague.*

English films have never been as dazzling as those of the more innovative French and Italian directors, but a number of excellent movies emanated from the British studios in the years after World War II. Adaptations of novels and plays, suspense dramas, and modestly budgeted but hugely amusing comedies were the three genres that proved most rewarding. Laurence Olivier followed his masterful *Henry V* with highly praised film versions of *Hamlet* and *Richard III.* Anthony Asquith directed *The Browning Version* with Michael Redgrave, *The Winslow Boy* with Robert Donat, and *The Importance of Being Earnest* with Edith Evans as a delightful Lady Bracknell. From David Lean, a meticulous, painstaking director, came two good films based on Dickens, *Great Expectations* and *Oliver Twist,* and a string of successful dramas, among them *Breaking the Sound Barrier* with Ralph Richardson and the romantic *Summertime* with Katharine Hepburn. He then turned to a series of expensive, American-financed "prestige" films, the best of which were *The Bridge on the River Kwai* (1957), in which Alec Guinness gave a great performance as an unbalanced British colonel in a Japanese prison camp in Burma, and *Lawrence of Arabia,* a gripping desert epic that made Peter O'Toole an international star in 1962.

For a time, Carol Reed rivaled Hitchcock as the master of suspense films. *Odd Man Out,* with James Mason as an escaped political prisoner on the run in Ireland; *The Fallen Idol,* about a young boy who thinks he sees a murder being committed; and *The Third Man,* a thriller set in postwar Vienna that culminates in a chase through the city's sewers, were among the most entertaining movies of the postwar period.

To many moviegoers on both sides of the Atlantic, however, the real jewels of the English cinema were its marvelous comedies, many of which emanated from Michael Balcon's Ealing Studios. Peculiarly English, these irresistible films were peopled by a gallery of eccentrics and often dealt with backwater groups who refused to knuckle under to the heartless bureaucracy of modern government. Among the best of these comedies were *Hue and Cry, Tight Little Island, I'm All Right Jack, School for Scoundrels,* and a wonderful series of films starring Alec Guinness: *Kind Hearts and Coronets,* in which Guinness plays nine murder victims in one family; *The Lavender Hill Mob,* in which he portrays a lisping bank clerk plotting larceny; and *Man in the White*

Suit, in which he discovers a new kind of cloth that will never wear out—much to the dismay of clothing manufacturers.

In the late 1950's, as the new wave was beginning to make itself felt in France, another group of young Turks was preparing to make its mark on the British cinema. British films, these young directors felt, were sentimental and unreal; the emphasis was on style and on impeccable acting, not on content that was relevant to the lives of contemporary Englishmen. Just as John Osborne, Harold Pinter, and others were revitalizing the theater, young film-makers began to focus on working-class men and women who raged against a social order that seemed totally antiquated. In Jack Clayton's *Room at the Top,* for example, Laurence Harvey plays an opportunistic young executive who finds security if not happiness by marrying a millionaire's daughter. In Tony Richardson's version of John Osborne's play *Look Back in Anger,* Richard Burton is superb as the archetypal "angry young man." And in Karel Reisz's *Saturday Night and Sunday Morning,* Albert Finney

The French made directors' films in the 1960's; the English made actors' films. These include The Servant *(top), a superb Pinter-Losey collaboration built around Dirk Bogarde's tour de force performance, and* A Taste of Honey *(right), with Rita Tushingham. Others (from left to right above), in ascending order of production cost: Richardson's* Look Back in Anger, *with Mary Ure and Richard Burton;* Bridge on the River Kwai, *which won Oscars for actor Alec Guinness and director David Lean; and* Lawrence of Arabia, *actor Peter O'Toole's greatest role.*

etches a memorable portrait of a virile young factory worker torn between two loves. Laurence Olivier gives one of his finest performances in Richardson's film from John Osborne's play *The Entertainer*, a searing drama about a third-rate music-hall performer and his family who are caught up in the social upheaval that marks the dissolution of the British Empire.

Joseph Stalin's death in 1953 temporarily ushered in a new period of achievement in the Russian cinema, one that had been stifled by government insistence on "social realism." Toward the close of the decade several remarkable Russian films were seen in the West. Grigori Chukhrai followed *The Forty-First*, a romance set during the revolution, with 1959's *Ballad of a Soldier*, a lovely, thoroughly engaging film about a young Russian signalman's experiences during a brief leave

from the World War II battlefield. *The Cranes Are Flying*, directed by Mikhaïl Kalatazov, was an exquisite film about a young girl in love.

Of the Communist satellites, Poland was the most productive in terms of interesting cinema. Certainly the most masterful Polish director was Andrzej Wajda, who received his initial training in a government film school and then went on to create a notable trio of films: *A Generation* and *Kanal*, which dealt with youthful Poles in the anti-German resistance movement during World War II, and *Ashes and Diamonds*, a dazzling drama about a political extremist who is asked to assassinate a government official. Wajda's growing technical skill was accompanied by an increasingly personal style that relied heavily on symbolism. Another noteworthy Polish director was Roman Polanski, whose first feature, *The Knife in the Water*, was a fascinating film about the triangular relationship of a yacht owner, his wife, and a young man.

Japan had long had a thriving film industry, but it was not until 1951, when the government reluctantly entered Akira Kurosawa's mas-

terpiece, *Rashomon*, in the Venice Film Festival, that the Western world was made aware of the stunning artistry of Japanese film-makers. During the 1950's, international audiences came to know and admire such great Japanese directors as Kenji Mizoguchi, creator of *Ugetsu Monogatari* and other powerful dramas set in medieval Japan; Teinosuke Kinugasa, director of the exquisite *Gate of Hell*; and Kon Ichikawa, whose *The Burmese Harp* and *Fires on the Plain*, set during World War II, were stinging commentaries on the barbarism of war. The low-key, tender films of Yasujiro Ozu, on the other hand, had little distribution abroad. His affectionate portraits of middle-class Japanese life were discovered by American critics in the 1970's, when such films as *Tokyo Story* (1953) and *An Autumn Afternoon* (1961) received belated acclaim.

There was certainly no delay in praising the films of Kurosawa, who was immediately recognized as one of the world's great film-makers. His films range from costume dramas (*The Throne of Blood*) to adaptions of Western classics (*The Idiot, The Lower Depths*) to dramas set in modern Japan (*High and Low*). Many of these films feature Toshiro Mifune, whose magnetism and expressive eyes make him the first Japanese actor to achieve international stardom.

Despite subsequent achievements, *Rashomon* remains Kurosawa's most famous film. It recounts—from four different points of view—what happens one day in a Japanese forest: a man and his wife meet a bandit who has sexual relations with the wife; later the husband dies. But was the wife raped, or did she submit willingly? Was the husband murdered, or did he commit suicide? The wife, the bandit, the husband (speaking through a medium), and a woodcutter who witnessed the event all tell their versions to the police, but the stories differ widely and the truth remains elusive.

The past two decades have witnessed the emergence of Japan, India, Israel, Czechoslovakia, Cuba, and Brazil as vital new centers of film culture, and they have seen the evolution of a new spirit of internationalism in film-making. The greatest of these national cinemas, the Japanese, had no foreign following until 1951, when Akira Kurosawa's Rashomon *(left) created a sensation at the Cannes Film Festival. Soon thereafter, a Bengali named Satyajit Ray released* Pather Panchali, *at right, and made the ethnic cinema of India a force to reckon with.*

Some critics, while acknowledging the greatness of *Rashomon*, regard *Seven Samurai*, a 1954 film about seven killers hired to defend a village from bandits, as Kurosawa's best. "Kurosawa is perhaps the greatest of all contemporary film craftsmen," wrote Pauline Kael, who praised "his use of the horizon for compositional variety, the seemingly infinite camera angles, the compositions that are alive with action, the almost abstract use of trees, flowers, sky, rain, mud, and moving figures. . . ." She went on to acclaim the film as the "greatest battle epic since 'The Birth of a Nation,'" calling it "a raging, sensuous work of such overpowering immediacy that it leaves you both exhilarated and exhausted."

The fireworks of Kurosawa films such as *Seven Samurai* are in marked contrast to the quiet dignity of Satyajit Ray's films, although Ray is also regarded by many critics as one of the world's great directors. The Indian film-maker's Apu Trilogy, three films about Bengali life, were hailed as a national epic in the 1950's. *Pather Panchali* is the story of a Bengali family's noble struggle against poverty and the heartbreaks of life. In *Aparajito* the son of the family grows to manhood. And in *The World of Apu* he marries, fails at his life's ambitions, and then, after losing his wife in childbirth, wanders across the country for several years before returning to claim his son. Some critics have been less than enthusiastic about Ray's work and have termed his films tedious, and his movies have never been popular in India itself, but those who appreciate his unobtrusive technique and his compassion for his characters view his films as a superb, poetic record of Indian life.

Today the films of Swedish director Ingmar Bergman win almost unanimous praise, but in the 1950's he too had many detractors among critics. Although few disputed his brilliant visual sense and his ability to elicit excellent performances from his company of expert players, his films seemed to many reviewers to be highly uneven and smothered by a "pall of profundity." Other critics, needless to say, endorsed his films wholeheartedly.

Bergman, the son of a strict Lutheran minister, directed his first film in 1945, and over the next several years he made a number of solemn dramas probing the relationship between men and women in love. He also made several lighter films, including the sophisticated and sardonic *Smiles of a Summer Night*. Then, in the mid-1950's, he began a series of dark, brooding films about the nature of good and evil, about faith and death, about the psychological and spiritual torment of mankind. In *The Seventh Seal*, a medieval knight plays chess with Death while he seeks the meaning of life. The scenes depicting the burning of a young witch, the masochism of a procession of flagellants, and the suffering of plague victims constitute an unforgettable visualization of the wretched condition of the human race. But in the end, the knight manages to

save from death a family of strolling players—a father, mother, and infant who are obviously symbols of Christianity. This striking allegory, which established Bergman's international reputation, is still regarded as one of his best films.

In Bergman's *Wild Strawberries*, Victor Seastrom, the distinguished director of silent films, gives a wonderful performance as an elderly doctor who, after dreaming of his own death, reviews his whole life while traveling to a university where he is to receive an honorary degree. In symbol-filled dream sequences and waking reveries, he relives his seventy-six years. *The Virgin Spring*, another film set in medieval times, sees evil overwhelm innocence as a young girl is raped and murdered; taking vengeance, her father kills not only the two murderers but also a guiltless boy who witnessed the crime. Afterward, a spring bubbles up from the spot on which the murder occurred.

Bergman's films, filled with unforgettable images, soaring lyricism, and an endless parade of earthly horrors and suffering, comprise a uniquely personal vision, and even those who find his films self-indulgent and flawed recognize his extraordinary talent. "When Bergman fails," Stanley Kauffmann wrote in 1960, "he does it at a level quite beyond most directors' successes."

What D.W. Griffith was to the silent cinema, Swedish director Ingmar Bergman is to modern film-making—an uncompromising craftsman, a visionary artist, and a dour prophet. Some highlights of his cinematic odyssey, clockwise from the left: Death, the last piper, from The Seventh Seal; *Victor Seastrom, supreme in old age, from* Wild Strawberries; *and innocence despoiled,* The Virgin Spring. *Above: uncanny resemblance, intertwined psyches, from* Persona.

10

New Talent, New Audience

DAY FOR NIGHT, which has been acclaimed as the best film of 1973, is François Truffaut's valentine to the movies. A lovely work about the making of a movie, it is permeated with Truffaut's affection for the self-centered, eccentric, talented people who create cinema, and it demonstrates that even in an era of greatly reduced movie attendance, film-making remains a uniquely glamorous and rewarding occupation.

Dedicated to Lillian and Dorothy Gish, Truffaut's film is filled with direct and indirect tributes to key movie-makers of the past and present. In one scene the director of the film-within-a-film—Truffaut himself—slowly unpacks a box of books, each of which deals with the career of a prominent director: Hawks, Welles, Hitchcock, Dreyer, Bresson, Godard, Bergman, and Rossellini. In another sequence the director, sleeping fitfully, dreams of an incident from his childhood involving the theft from a movie theater of still photographs from the current attraction, *Citizen Kane*. Later, a crowd of film workers is asked to make murmuring noises for a sound track, but they must be warned not to talk about movies.

For the young, movies were a stimulating and provocative art form throughout the sixties and early seventies. Older generations, on the other hand, abandoned moviegoing in favor of television. Most people over thirty went to the movies rarely and saw only the one or two blockbusters that were released each year, enormously successful films like *The Godfather* and *The Sound of Music*, each of which earned its studio more than eighty million dollars in North America alone. The habit of regular moviegoing had been lost, and the cinema, once entertainment for the masses, had become diversion for the few.

Hollywood, long the dominant center of the movies, became a ghost town, with television providing the only jobs for once regularly employed movie-makers. There were still feature films being made, of course, but there were woefully few of them in comparison to the golden years of the forties, and most were being filmed in Europe where costs were lower or on location where directors found opportunities for verisimilitude and freedom from studio interference. The old studio executives were replaced by cost-conscious businessmen who cut payrolls drastically, sold off the studio acreage for real-estate developments, and even auctioned off the great collections of props that had appeared in scores of movies over the years.

By the early 1970's, critics and fans alike had come to regard the cinema more as an art form than as a form of entertainment. Increasingly, movies were made to appeal to an enthusiastic but circumscribed audience of film buffs, many of them under the age of thirty. Cinema as art stirred many of the controversies traditionally associated with new modes of artistic expression, a situation exemplified by the furore attending the first screenings of Bernardo Bertolucci's Last Tango in Paris *(opposite).*

Seeking a panacea, the studio chiefs tried many approaches. They paid millions of dollars to a handful of big stars until it became apparent that audiences would no longer pay to see most stars if their vehicles weren't good. Big-budget spectaculars and musicals brought several studios to the brink of bankruptcy and made it clear that size and extravagance were no substitutes for taste and talent. When *Easy Rider*, a low-budget "road movie" of the late 1960's, netted huge profits, the studios produced a deluge of low-budget films made by young directors. The result was a score of flops spurned by the young audiences the films were designed to attract. The success of foreign films offering nudity and simulated sex prompted Hollywood's film-makers to squeeze as much nudity as possible into their pictures, but their efforts were largely overshadowed by independently produced hardcore pornography. The result of this trend was a backlash reflected in a 1973 Supreme Court decision that reopened the troublesome issue of local censorship of films. By the mid-seventies, therefore, it seemed safer to eschew vivid sex in favor of mayhem and brutality, although more thoughtful moviegoers concluded that violent films were more harmful to society than sexy ones.

The Hollywood studios that managed to produce one or two gigantic moneymakers every few years were able to survive, but debt-ridden, ill-starred MGM, once the most glamorous and powerful of all, announced in 1973 that it would no longer distribute films; MGM would continue to produce some movies, but they would be released by other companies while MGM concentrated on television projects and on its expensive new venture, the Grand Hotel in Las Vegas.

Partially filling the power vacuum left by the once-omnipotent studio moguls was a new breed of American directors. Of these, none was as consistently successful as Stanley Kubrick, whose controversial films made so much money that studios were happy to put up capital for Kubrick's new films without even knowing what the plot was to be. The director demonstrated his versatility and brilliance with *The Killing*, a hard-hitting, low-budget gangster film, in 1956; *Paths of Glory*, a highly effective antiwar film; *Spartacus*, the most intelligent of the big-budget spectacles; and 1962's *Lolita*, an uneven but rewarding adaptation of the Nabokov novel. It was, however, *Dr. Strangelove, or How I learned to stop worrying and love the Bomb* that put Kubrick's career in high gear in 1964. One of the best American films of the sixties, it is a scathing black comedy about the accidental advent of nuclear war. When an insane right-wing general launches an unauthorized attack on Russia, the appalled American President warns the Russians and implores them to shoot down the American bombers before they reach their targets. Despite the efforts of all concerned, however, one plane does get through to discharge its bomb, and the film ends with scenes of atomic mushrooms. Although an unlikely subject for comedy, *Dr. Strangelove* proved to be both chilling and hilarious.

Kubrick's next release was *2001: A Space Odyssey*, a science fiction film that made a fortune despite its rather obscure story line. Young audiences in particular found it fascinating, with its millions of dollars worth of machinery, its superb special effects, and its exquisite evocation of the mystery and beauty of outer space. *A Clockwork Orange*,

which followed in 1972, was a horrifying vision of the unbridled violence of society in the near future.

Another remarkable talent was Arthur Penn, director of 1967's *Bonnie and Clyde*. Suggested by the real-life careers of Clyde Barrow and Bonnie Parker, who entered American folklore after committing a series of highly publicized bank robberies during the Depression, the film daringly combined comedy and violence, horror and nostalgia, and culminated in a seemingly endless slow-motion sequence in which Bonnie (Faye Dunaway) and Clyde (Warren Beatty) were riddled with bullets. Condemned by some reviewers, it was nevertheless a film that seemed justified in its use of explicit brutality because the result was a powerful comment on the nature of violence.

Mike Nichols, fresh from an unbroken string of Broadway successes, turned to films in 1966 with *Who's Afraid of Virginia Woolf?* and then made one of the decade's biggest hits, *The Graduate*. The tale of a bemused young man (Dustin Hoffman) repelled by the hypocrisy and materialism of his parents' generation, who has an affair with an older woman (Anne Bancroft) and then falls in love with her daughter, it made Nichols one of the most sought-after American directors. Another important new talent was Peter Bogdanovitch, who, like Truffaut, has been obsessed with movies from early childhood. His 1971 offering, *The Last Picture Show*, was a powerful drama about an adolescent boy's transition to manhood in a dusty Texas hamlet.

William Friedkin came to prominence with *The French Connection*, a tough, exciting film about an irreverent New York detective's pursuit of an international narcotics gang. Friedkin's film version of *The Exorcist*, released late in 1973, quickly became one of the biggest moneymakers in movie history. Francis Ford Coppola, a scriptwriter and director, was the guiding hand behind the movie version of another best seller, *The Godfather*, which won critical acclaim in 1972, returned Marlon Brando to the ranks of top stars, and enriched Paramount beyond that studio's wildest expectations. Robert Altman's *M*A*S*H*, a black comedy about an army medical unit during the Korean War, was both a critical and a financial success, although his later films were more popular with critics than with the public.

The most appealing new talents in comedy were Woody Allen and Elaine May, both of whom were performers as well as directors. Allen, epitome of the meek urban "schnook," revealed in such films as *Bananas* and *Sleeper* a wild comic imagination and an irresistible screen presence. May, one of the few women directors to make a mark in American films, brought to *A New Leaf* and *The Heartbreak Kid* a perceptive and deliciously malicious view of modern life.

The 1960's were not a fruitful period for that American specialty, the musical film. Robert Wise's film versions of *West Side Story* and *The Sound of Music* and George Cukor's adaptation of *My Fair Lady* were hugely profitable, however, as were *Mary Poppins* and *Funny Girl*. But the best musical of the period was probably *Cabaret*, a dazzling film that was brilliantly directed by Bob Fosse and superbly performed by Liza Minnelli and Joel Grey.

Liza, the talented daughter of Judy Garland and Vincente Minnelli,

Fickle audiences, falling revenues, and skyrocketing production costs created new dilemmas for Hollywood in the 1960's. The success of My Fair Lady *(left above) and* The Sound of Music *(left) notwithstanding, the days of the surefire moneymaker were over. The success of low-budget movies like* Easy Rider *(below) seemed to suggest that the public preferred unpolished, personalized film making. Then came* The Godfather *(above), a powerful rebuke to those who claimed that Hollywood was dead.*

was proof that the star system, despite reports to the contrary, was still very much alive. The demise of long-term studio contracts ended the careers of many stars, to be sure, and most of those still in demand were forced to take a percentage of eventual profits in lieu of big salaries, but the truly popular stars reaped tremendous rewards. Marlon Brando reportedly earned one and a half million dollars from his share of *The Godfather* profits and more than three million dollars from his piece of *Last Tango in Paris*.

The heir to Gable's crown was Paul Newman, a blue-eyed, good-looking performer whose irreverence audiences found especially attractive. He became a star in the late 1950's in such films as *Somebody Up There Likes Me* and *Cat on a Hot Tin Roof* and proved throughout the 1960's—in *The Hustler, Hud, Cool Hand Luke,* and other movies—that he was a capable actor as well as a true star personality. In 1968 he directed his wife, Joanne Woodward, in *Rachel, Rachel* and won the New York Film Critics' award as best director of the year. Richard Burton, a fine Welsh actor, suddenly found himself a major star when he and Elizabeth Taylor became the most publicized romantic duo since Edward VIII and Wallis Simpson. Taylor and Burton were costars in the forty-million-dollar epic *Cleopatra*, which almost bankrupted Twentieth Century Fox. By contrast, the brutal "spaghetti Westerns" that made Clint Eastwood a top box-office attraction were filmed in Italy on very low budgets. Eastwood returned to America in triumph and now specializes in violent Westerns and detective films.

Steve McQueen reached stardom by portraying grown-up delinquents whose guts and determination enabled them to emerge victorious from all sorts of predicaments. He is the fast, tough, modern hero par excellence, as demonstrated in such films as *The Great Escape* and *Bullitt*. A late starter was gifted George C. Scott, who attained superstar status portraying George Patton in Franklin Schaffner's popular film biography of that World War II general. A star of a far different stripe was Dustin Hoffman, who drew critical raves for *The Graduate* and then proved his versatility with a superb performance as a tubercular derelict in *Midnight Cowboy*. The first black performer to become a romantic hero in films was Sidney Poitier, whose fans flocked to *In the Heat of the Night, Lilies of the Field,* and *Guess Who's Coming to Dinner?* A more conventional movie idol was Robert Redford, a handsome blond actor who proved to be a major box-office attraction in *Butch Cassidy and the Sundance Kid* and *The Sting* (both with Paul Newman), *The Way We Were,* and *The Great Gatsby*.

The sixties and early seventies were lean periods for women, for whom few important roles were written. There were brilliant performances by Patricia Neal in *Hud,* Anne Bancroft in *The Miracle Worker* and *The Graduate,* and Geraldine Page in *Sweet Bird of Youth,* but none of those actresses worked in films with any regularity. Joanne Woodward was more active, winning plaudits for such vehicles as *Rachel, Rachel* and *Summer Wishes, Winter Dreams*. The most important new dramatic discovery of the late 1960's was undoubtedly Jane Fonda, who revealed in *They Shoot Horses, Don't They?* and *Klute* that she was a natural actress of great potential.

Success did not spoil Federico Fellini, but it did permit him to indulge his innermost fantasies. The result was a series of film phantasmagorias, part autobiography and part daydream. The most memorable of these was 8½ (below), a montage of real and imagined incidents in the director's life. This was followed in 1969 by a wildly improvisational film version of the Satyricon *that was one part Petronius and three parts Fellini (right).*

Doris Day's successor as box-office queen was Julie Andrews, a likable singing actress whose performances in *Mary Poppins* and *The Sound of Music* elevated her to stardom. Her successor in turn was Barbra Streisand, who has almost more talent than the screen can hold. She has starred in musicals like *Funny Girl* and *Hello, Dolly* and in a series of comedies and dramas that have earned enormous sums.

Early in 1974, it was announced that Streisand would star in Ingmar Bergman's next film, a remake of *The Merry Widow*. It was interesting news but hardly startling in an era when performers and directors ignored international boundaries and willingly worked wherever there was a potentially rewarding project. The English film industry typified this trend, with British artists working all over the world and talent from everywhere coming to England to work. Among the top "British" films of the 1960's were *The Servant* by Joseph Losey, an American; *Morgan* by a Czech, Karel Reisz; Antonioni's *Blow-up*, and Silvio Narizzano's *Georgy Girl*. "American" films made by British directors included *Deliverance* by John Boorman, *Bullitt* by Peter Yates, *Midnight Cowboy* by John Schlesinger, and David Lean's *Dr. Zhivago*.

Schlesinger was probably the most successful of the new British directors. *Darling*, released in 1965, was a scalding portrait of an ambitious young woman (Julie Christie) who claws her way to the top of the amoral jet set. *Midnight Cowboy*, which won Schlesinger an Oscar in 1969, was an affecting movie about the relationship between two of society's rejects, movingly portrayed by Dustin Hoffman and Jon Voight. And *Sunday, Bloody Sunday* was an unusually compelling and intelligent movie about a divorcee (Glenda Jackson), a doctor (Peter Finch), and the young man they both love.

Richard Lester was another influential British director. Master of

quick cuts and flashy editing, he made two entertaining films with the Beatles, *Help!* and *A Hard Day's Night*, both of which captured the Liverpool quartet's charm and iconoclasm. A very different type of comedy, but equally popular, was Tony Richardson's funny, bawdy, and beautiful film version of Fielding's *Tom Jones*. The highlight of the film was the famous eating scene with Albert Finney and Joyce Redman; as William Bayer has pointed out, "their devouring of food is so erotic that the scene outclasses, on a purely sensual level, any of the frank, nude lovemaking scenes which began to appear on the screen in the 1970's."

Joseph Losey, who had worked abroad since the days of the Hollywood blacklist, directed a series of fascinating and visually beautiful films in England during the 1960's. Three of them—*The Servant, Accident*, and *The Go-Between*—had scripts by Harold Pinter. *The Servant* in particular was unforgettable; Dirk Bogarde was superb as a corrupt manservant who gradually assumes total control over his young master (James Fox), whom he drives to the depths of degradation and despair.

While Paul Scofield, who played Thomas More in Fred Zinnemann's film version of *A Man for All Seasons*, and Rex Harrison, who starred in *My Fair Lady*, were winning new laurels in American films, a new crop of British actors was emerging. Peter O'Toole, Albert Finney, Michael Caine, Alan Bates, Richard Harris, Terence Stamp, and Michael York all became international stars, while Sean Connery became a multimillionaire and a folk hero thanks to his impersonation of Ian Fleming's James Bond in a series of incredibly popular films. Maggie Smith, Rita Tushingham, Lynn Redgrave, and Julie Christie

Working outside the studio system and independent of budgets and deadlines, Stanley Kubrick has produced a dozen films— each an important contribution to cinema history and each a reaffirmation of his immense talent. In addition to Paths of Glory, Lolita, *and* Doctor Strangelove, *his credits include* 2001: A Space Odyssey, *an exercise in cinema technology (right), and.* A Clockwork Orange *(left above), a repellent portrait of tomorrow's society.*

were prominent new female stars, although the two most exciting young British actresses were undoubtedly Glenda Jackson, whose potential seemed unlimited, and Vanessa Redgrave, who combined enormous talent with great beauty.

Blow-up, released in 1966, was a tremendous commercial success for the controversial Italian director, whose post-*L'Avventura* films (*La Notte, L'Eclisse, The Red Desert*) had received critical acclaim but limited patronage. Featuring David Hemmings as a high fashion photographer who may or may not have witnessed and photographed a murder taking place in a London park, *Blow-up* is a fascinating study of the restless, valueless life-style of "swinging London's" pacesetters.

Federico Fellini, the other major Italian director, continued to create bizarre, highly personal films that were lavishly produced and immensely entertaining. *8½*, so named because he had previously made six films and parts of three others, is regarded as one of Fellini's best. Obviously autobiographical, the 1963 film stars Marcello Mastroianni as a movie director suffering from creative block. Among the most vivid scenes are an orgy in a wine vat, an interview with a cardinal in a subterranean steam bath, and a sequence in which the director pictures himself as the master of a harem, cracking a whip over all the various women who have been important in his life.

From Luchino Visconti came several ornate, operatic films that ranged from the elegaic *The Leopard* to *The Damned*, a stunning saga about a family of depraved German aristocrats during the Nazi era. Vittorio de Sica's *Garden of the Finzi-Continis*, Pietro Germi's *Seduced and Abandoned*, Elio Petri's *Investigation of a Citizen above Suspicion*, Mario Monicelli's *Big Deal on Madonna Street*, and Dino Risi's *The Easy Life* were all international successes, while the films of Pier Paolo Pasolini, including *The Gospel According to St. Matthew* and *Teorema*, won praise from some critics. Gillo Pontecorvo's *Battle of Algiers*, filmed in documentary style, was phenomenally powerful.

In the late 1970's, the strikingly talented Bernardo Bertolucci burst upon the international scene with the controversial *Last Tango in Paris*, in which Marlon Brando gave one of his finest performances. It was, in short, a film about sex and the way that human beings use sex as a refuge, a release, and a weapon. The frank dialogue, the nudity, and the simulated sex were not gratuitously employed but were integral to the theme of the film, and if the picture was not totally successful, it was certainly unforgettable.

In France, François Truffaut embellished his already exalted reputation with a string of new successes: the autobiographical *Stolen Kisses* and *Bed and Board*; *The Bride Wore Black*, his homage to Hitchcock; the powerful *The Wild Child*; and, of course, the enchanting *Day for Night*. Jean-Luc Godard, who made at least two films a year, remained enormously influential although his films became more and more political and his audiences shrank accordingly. One of his most bitter films was *Weekend*, released in 1967. An attack on middle-class materialism, it deals with a greedy couple who, as Pauline Kael summarizes it, "wreck their car, and as they wander the highways, lost among battered cars and bleeding dead . . . have a series of picaresque adventures, encountering figures from literature and from films, until they meet a new race of hippie guerrillas—revolutionary cannibals raping and feeding on the bourgeoisie." Kael goes on to say that despite the film's weakness, "the nightmarish anger that seems to cry out for a revolution of total destruction and the visionary lyricism are so strong they hold the movie together. . . . It's possible to hate half or two-thirds of what Godard does . . . and still be shattered by his brilliance."

From Alain Resnais in 1966 came *La Guerre est Finie*, starring Yves Montand as a Spanish revolutionary who returns illegally to his native country after a period of exile. Eric Rohmer's cerebral "moral tales," including *My Night at Maude's, Claire's Knee,* and *Chloe in the Afternoon,* were acclaimed by critics everywhere, as were Claude Chabrol's psychologically oriented studies of murders and their aftereffects: *La Femme Infidèle, Le Boucher,* and *Que la Bête Meure. Au Hasard, Balthasar,* and *Une Femme Douce* were further manifestations of Robert Bresson's unique personal vision, while *Playtime* and *Traffic* were new products of Jacques Tati's comic genius.

From Costa-Gavras, a director of Russo-Greek origins who grew up in France, came three suspenseful dramas inspired by contemporary political situations. *Z* was a dazzlingly effective film about a political assassination in Greece; *The Confession* was set in Prague during the purge of 1951; while *State of Siege* dealt with the kidnapping of an American diplomat by South American revolutionaries.

The greatest Spanish director was still, of course, Luis Buñuel, although he worked primarily in Mexico and France and the few films he actually made in his native land were eventually banned there for their anticlericism. His films of the 1960's included *Viridiana,* which, with the director's typical blend of realism, surrealism, and horror, told of the fruitless attempt of a convent-reared girl to live a godly life on the outside; *Exterminating Angel,* in which guests at a party find themselves unwilling to leave and so remain there, becoming increasingly miserable; and two superb films with the exquisite French actress Catherine Deneuve. In *Belle de Jour* she plays an elegant, bored housewife who spends her free time working in an expensive bordello (or does she just imagine it?—one is never quite sure), while in *Tristana* she portrays a girl who is seduced by her guardian and runs away but after losing a leg to cancer cynically weds him and inherits his wealth.

The sixties and early seventies were also a rich period for Ingmar Bergman. *The Silence, Persona, Hour of the Wolf, The Shame, A Passion,* and *Cries and Whispers* were all marked by Bergman's deep pessimism and by a continuous probing into the souls of human beings in anguish. Bergman films were harrowing experiences for moviegoers, but his ever-increasing artistry made them unforgettable. Although Bergman was obviously in a class by himself, he was not the only Scandinavian film-maker of note. Jan Troell emerged as an important new talent with two beautiful films, *The Emigrants* and *The New Land,* which featured Liv Ullmann and Max von Sydow as a Swedish couple who make a new life for themselves in America.

It was not, for the most part, a rich period for Russian films. Among the few Soviet movies seen in the West were Sergei Bondar-

chuk's lavish, eight-hour adaptation of *War and Peace* and Grigori Kozintsev's *Hamlet*. The direct correlation between artistic freedom and artistic achievement was proven again in Czechoslovakia, which experienced a brief cinematic renaissance that produced a number of remarkable films before the Russian invasion of that country in 1968 restored a repressive regime. Jan Kadar's *Shop on Main Street*, Milós Forman's *The Loves of a Blonde*, and Jiri Menzel's *Closely Watched Trains* merited and received international admiration. Other notable film-makers from Communist nations included Istvan Szabo and Karoly Makk from Hungary and Cuba's Tomás Gutierrez Alea, whose *Memories of Underdevelopment* won critical superlatives.

Early in 1974, an article in *The New York Times* reported that the interest in cinema among young people was still increasing. In the United States alone, some 24,000 students were taking courses in film-making and film history at more than six hundred colleges. To these students and their counterparts around the world, film is the most exciting of art forms, the one most relevant to their generation. Their enthusiasm for films ranging from old Bogart movies to the latest underground epic from Andy Warhol and the newest Fellini is heartening to those who love the movies, for from their ranks may well emerge the film-makers of the future. The successful debuts of such talented young American directors as Martin Scorsese (*Mean Streets*), George Lucas (*American Graffiti*), Terrence Malick (*Badlands*), and Steven Spielberg (*The Sugarland Express*) are proof of the vitality and excitement that new talent can provide.

Even more welcome were reports that movie attendance had increased dramatically in late 1973 and the first part of 1974. The rise in box-office receipts was partly attributable to the appeal of several blockbuster attractions, partly to the gasoline shortage, which kept people close to home. But it was also clear that many people were rediscovering how enjoyable going out to the movies could be.

It is unlikely that moviegoing will ever become the weekly habit it once was for millions. There is, however, an international audience hungry for good films, and as long as that is so there will be movie-makers anxious to entertain and edify them, move them to tears, and gladden their hearts with laughter.

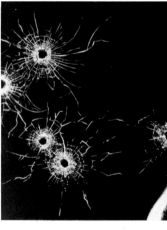

MAKING
THE MOVIES

Perhaps the most famous character in the history of film comedy is Charles Chaplin's "The Little Tramp." No one, including Chaplin, could have predicted the character's longevity when it was created on the set of a Mack Sennett film in 1914.

The day after I finished [shooting a picture] with [Henry] Lehrman, Sennett returned from location. Ford Sterling was on one set, Arbuckle on another; the whole stage was crowded with three companies at work. I was in my street clothes and had nothing to do, so I stood where Sennett could see me. He was standing with Mabel [Normand], looking into a hotel lobby set, biting the end of a cigar. "We need some gags here," he said, then turned to me. "Put on a comedy make-up. Anything will do."

I had no idea what make-up to put on. I did not like my getup as the press reporter. However, on the way to the wardrobe I thought I would dress in baggy pants, big shoes, a cane and a derby hat. I wanted everything a contradiction: the pants baggy, the coat tight, the hat small and the shoes large. I was undecided whether to look old or young, but remembering Sennett had expected me to be a much older man, I added a small mustache, which, I reasoned, would add age without hiding my expression.

I had no idea of the character. But the moment I was dressed, the clothes and the make-up made me feel the person he was. I began to know him, and by the time I walked onto the stage he was fully born. When I confronted Sennett I assumed the character and strutted about, swinging my cane and parading before him. Gags and comedy ideas went racing through my mind.

The secret of Mack Sennett's success was his enthusiasm. He was a great audience and laughed genuinely at what he thought funny. He stood and giggled until his body began to shake. This encouraged me and I began to explain that character: "You know this fellow is many-sided, a tramp, a gentleman, a poet, a dreamer, a lonely fellow, always hopeful of romance and adventure. He would have you believe he is a scientist, a musician, a duke, a polo player. However, he is not above picking up cigarette butts or robbing a baby of its candy. And, of course, if the occasion warrants it, he will kick a lady in the rear—but only in extreme anger!"

I carried on this way for ten minutes or more, keeping Sennett in continuous chuckles. "All right," said he, "get on the set and see what you can do there." As with the Lehrman film, I knew little of what the story was about, other than that Mabel Normand gets involved with her husband and a lover.

In all comedy business an attitude is most important, but it is not always easy to find an attitude. However, in the hotel lobby I felt I was an imposter posing as one of the guests, but in reality I was a tramp just wanting a little shelter. I entered and stumbled over the foot of a lady. I turned and raised my hat apologetically, then turned and stumbled

over a cuspidor, then turned and raised my hat to the cuspidor. Behind the camera they began to laugh.

Quite a crowd had gathered there, not only the players of the other companies who left their sets to watch us, but also the stagehands, the carpenters and the wardrobe department. That indeed was a compliment. And by the time we had finished rehearsing we had quite a large audience laughing. Very soon I saw Ford Sterling peering over the shoulders of others. When it was over I knew I had made good.

At the end of the day when I went to the dressing room, Ford Sterling and Roscoe Arbuckle were taking off their make-up. Very little was said, but the atmosphere was charged with crosscurrents. Both Ford and Roscoe liked me, but I frankly felt they were undergoing some inner conflict.

It was a long scene that ran seventy-five feet. Later Mr. Sennett and Mr. Lehrman debated whether to let it run its full length, as the average comedy scene rarely ran over ten. "If it's funny," I said, "does length really matter?" They decided to let the scene run its full seventy-five feet. As the clothes had imbued me with the character, I then and there decided I would keep to this costume, whatever happened.

That evening I went home on the streetcar with one of the small-bit players. Said he, "Boy, you've started something; nobody ever got those kind of laughs on the set before, not even Ford Sterling—and you should have seen his face watching you, it was a study!"

"Let's hope they'll laugh the same way in the theatre," I said, by way of suppressing my elation.

CHARLES CHAPLIN
My Autobiography, 1964

Under conditions that seem primitive by comparison with today's highly mechanized film-making techniques, D. W. Griffith produced the complex and innovative films that form a vital part of our movie history. Lillian Gish, a frequent star in Griffith's films and a trusted collaborator, recreates the spirit of experimentation that existed during the filming of The Birth of a Nation.

As always, sunlight controlled the shooting schedule. Preparations began at five or six in the morning. The actors rose at five in order to be ready at seven, when it was bright enough for filming. Important scenes were played in the hard noon sun. I remember that we used to beg to have our closeups taken just after dawn or before sunset, as the soft yellow glow was easier to work in and much more flattering. We continued to work—often without a break for lunch—until sundown.

At that time young actors were learning not only to act but also to direct. When they weren't acting, George Siegmann and Bobby Harron served as assistant directors. All the young people, in fact, were at Mr. Griffith's elbow to help in any way that he chose to use them.

To economize, Mr. Griffith used many of the actors in more than one role. Bobby Harron, for instance, might play my brother in the morning, and in the afternoon put on blackface and play a Negro. . . . In the battle scenes several featured actors rode horses—but in the distance, well away from the camera. For many small roles, members of the company who happened to be working on other films came on the set of *The Birth* for a day or two.

The entire staff came on set to watch us, particularly Joe Aller and the men from the laboratory, so that they would know the effects that Mr. Griffith was seeking. This was of utmost importance, for each scene was shot only once. The only scene that was taken twice was the one in which Mae Marsh as the Little Sister leaps to her death from a cliff.

In those days there was no one to keep track of what an actor was wearing from scene to scene. He was obliged to remember for himself what he had worn and how his hair and makeup had looked in a previous scene. If he forgot, he was not used again. When the death scene was filmed, Mae forgot to tie the Confederate flag, which she'd been wearing in the previous scene, around her waist, and the scene had to be retaken. How we all envied her a second chance in a big moment!

In filming the battles, Mr. Griffith organized the action like a general. He stood at the top of a forty-foot tower, the commander-in-chief of both armies, his powerful voice, like Roarin' Jake's, thundering commands through a megaphone to his staff of assistants. Meetings were called before each major filmed sequence and a chain of command was developed from Mr. Griffith through his directors and their assistants. The last-in-command might have only four or five extras under him. These men, wearing uniforms and taking their places among the extras, also played parts in the film.

Griffith's camera was high on the platform looking down on the battle field, so that he could obtain a grand sweep of the action. This camera took the long shots. Hidden under bushes or in back of trees were cameras for closeups.

When the din of cannons, galloping horses, and charging men grew too great, no human voice, not even Mr. Griffith's, was powerful enough to be heard. Some of the extras were stationed as far as two miles from the camera. So a series of magnifying mirrors was used to flash signals to those actors working a great distance away. Each group of men had its number—one flash of the mirror for the first group, two for the second group, and so on. As group one started action, the mirror would flash a go-ahead to group two.

Care was taken to place the authentic old guns and the best horsemen in the first ranks. Other weapons, as well as poorer horsemen, were relegated to the background. Extras were painstakingly drilled in their parts until they knew when to charge, when to push cannons forward, when to fall.

Some of the artillery was loaded with real shells, and elaborate

warnings were broadcast about their range of fire. Mr. Griffith's sense of order and control made it possible for the cast and extras to survive the broiling heat, pounding hoofs, naked bayonets, and exploding shells without a single injury. He was too thoughtful of the welfare of others to permit accidents.

In most war films it is difficult to distinguish between the enemies unless the film is in color and the two sides are wearing different-colored uniforms. But not in a Griffith movie. Mr. Griffith had the rare technical skill to keep each side distinct and clear cut. In *The Birth*, the Confederate army always entered from the left of the camera, the Union army from the right.

One day he said to Billy, "I want to show a whole army moving."

"What do you mean, a whole army?" Bitzer [the cameraman] asked.

"Everyone we can muster."

"I'll have to move them back to get them all in view," Billy said. "They won't look much bigger than jackrabbits."

"That's all right. The audience will supply the details. Let's move up on this hill, Billy. Then we can shoot the whole valley and all the troops at once."

They never talked much, but they always seemed to understand each other. People around Mr. Griffith didn't bother him with idle talk.

When daylight disappeared, Mr. Griffith would order bonfires lit and film some amazing night scenes. Billy was pessimistic about the results; he kept insisting that they would be unsuccessful. But Mr. Griffith persisted. One big battle scene was filmed at night. The sub-title was to read, "It went on into the night." Nothing like it had ever been seen before. Those of us who had time were there—the women to watch, the men to help.

Although everything was carefully organized, whenever he saw a spontaneous gesture that looked good—like the soldier's leaning on his gun and looking at me during the hospital scene—he would call Billy over to film it.

In that scene, the wards were filled with wounded soldiers, and in the background nurses and orderlies attended their patients. In the doorway of the ward stood a Union sentry. As Elsie Stoneman, I was helping to entertain the wounded, singing and playing the banjo. The sentry watched me lovingly as I sang and then, after I had finished and was passing him, raised his hang-dog head and heaved a deep, love-sick sigh. The scene lasted only a minute, but it drew the biggest laugh of the film and became one of its best-remembered moments.

The scene came about in typical Griffith fashion. We players had no one to help us with our costumes. We had to carry our various changes to the set, as we could not afford the time to run back to our dressing rooms. Those period dresses, with their full skirts over hoops, were heavy. A kind young man who liked me helped me with my

props and costumes. The young man, William Freeman, was playing
the sentry, and he simply stood there, listening, as I sang. Seeing his
expression, Mr. Griffith said to Bitzer, "Billy, get that picture on film
right away." He knew that it would bring a laugh, which was needed
to break the dramatic tension.

LILLIAN GISH
Mr. Griffith, the Movies, and Me, 1969

*A large portion of the movies' magic stems from special effects created
by cameramen and technicians. Many of these feats are spectacular and
costly. But as recounted by Karl Brown, a cameraman for D. W.
Griffith in the early 1900's, the unusual can sometimes cost very little.*

Strange, weird, and impossible story ideas kept coming out of Frank
Wood's [Griffith's story editor] office. There was one, *The Flying
Torpedo,* that was so fantastically impossible that I doubt if Jules
Verne himself could have made it acceptable. Here it is: sometime in
the far-distant future our shores are being threatened by an unnamed
but terrible enemy. His fleet is already in battle array and firing salvo
after salvo of heavy shells to destroy our cities. What to do? Ah! Our
brave inventor comes up with a brilliant answer. Blast him out of the
water with guided missiles controlled by radio impulses.

Guided missiles indeed! Who ever heard of such a thing? And radio
impulses to boot. Ridiculous. H. G. Wells had supplied us with plenty
of science fiction like *The Invisible Man* and *The War of the Worlds,*
but they had been nothing like as hare-brained as this. However, the
man who brought the idea in, a fellow named McCarthy, was a sort of
radio nut himself, and he made it all sound so very convincing that the
company fell for it. So the idea was approved and put into production.
There was no trouble about the flying torpedo itself. Fireworks Wilson
[in charge of special effects] had been firing display rockets for years;
it was no trick at all for him to bury a rocket in a fancied-up conception of what a rocket might look like far in the future, and the thing
worked like a charm.

'There was no trouble about the bombardment destroying cities,
either. Fireworks Wilson himself stood on a high parallel and threw
contact-triggered torpedoes into the toy cities and scattered them high,
wide, and handsome. But when it came to getting shots of the enemy
battle fleet firing salvos from offshore, that was an entirely different
matter. There was no trouble about making up a fleet of toy battleships. Our carpenter shop could make anything. Fireworks Wilson
could fix the toy guns so they'd fire beautifully. The trouble was with
the water.

These toy battleships were set afloat in a shallow tank filled to the
brim with water. Since it was a night shot, black cotton velvet supplied
all the background that was needed. The lighting was held down, so

FAY W
ROBT. AF
BRUCE

there was just barely enough to get an image. This was all very good thinking, because the fakier the shot, the less you see of it the better. However, one thing could *not* be hidden. A tub of water is a tub of water, and little ripples are little ripples, and there's no getting around it. They shot it this way and they shot it that, but no matter how they shot it, the scene still looked like toy ships in a baby's bath.

I knew perfectly well that any old-line stage crew could lick a problem like that without half trying. For the art of stagecraft is the art of illusion, and our old-timers were quite literally magicians in this highly specialized line of work....

But even though I felt certain that the bombardment scene could be licked by going back to the first principles of stagecraft, I still hesitated about offering my ideas to McCarthy. He would probably tell me to go do something undignified to myself. So I went to Frank Woods and told him I thought there was a quick and easy way of getting the scene. He looked at me wearily and said, "Quick and easy, eh? That's what they've been telling us all along, how quick and easy everything was going to be. Know how much we've wasted on that one scene alone?" He paused to shake his head as he regretted the folly of ever under-taking such a picture in the first place. He pulled out of his slump to speak with resigned hopelessness as he said, "Well, I might as well know the worst now as later. How much is this going to cost us *this* time?"

"Well, I don't know much about the overhead, but—"

He cut me short with, "*Overhead!* Don't ever mention that word to me, it spoils my whole day. How much will it cost over the line?"

"Over the line?"

"Yes. How much over and above the fixed charges like salaries, transportation, film, and so on. How much for extra equipment?"

"Well, I'll have to fly a ground row as a teaser or tormenter—"

"Never mind the backstage lingo. We know you've been in the theater, you've mentioned it often enough. Now give it to me straight. How much actual dough?"

A personally directed
MERIAN C. **COOPER** ERNEST B. **SCHOEDSAC**
om the story by **PRODUCTION** Chief Technic
EDGAR WALLACE WILLIS I. O'BR
REO RADIO PICTURE
DAVID O. SELZNICK

I had to think for a moment and do a bit of counting on my fingers. Better to overstate and come in safe than to underguess and have to beg for more. "Well, I'd say about fifty cents, maybe sixty-five." He stared at me uncomprehendingly. I was quick to reassure him. "It won't go over that. If it does, I'll pay for it out of my own pocket, and that's a promise."

"As much as all that?" he asked, trying to be severely shocked and not succeeding. He thought it all over very carefully as though strug-gling with a momentous decision, and then said, "Tell you what I'll do. I'll accept that estimate and go you one better. Here's a whole dollar. Take it. Spend it. Don't stint yourself. Give it the works. Oh, and another thing. The details of this agreement must remain strictly between us. You're the only producer on the lot who has ever had the entire budget of his picture given to him cash in advance, and if it ever got out, they'd all be after me for the same thing. Understand?"

I said yes, sir, and got out of there before he could change his mind and want his dollar back.

Preparing the equipment was ridiculously easy. Cash Shockey painted a row of battleships in a line on a piece of compo-board six feet long. They were done in a nice, even, misty gray, the gray of things seen at a distance of five or more miles. The men in the carpenter shop profiled it for me, stiffened it with a strong batten, glued and nailed to the back so it wouldn't waver or wobble in the wind. They made me a pair of upright supports that would hold the profile of the ships at any desired height, and supplied C-clamps to hold it firmly in place. Fireworks Wilson gave me all the squibs I wanted and refused payment. These squibs, which were popular with children, were little paper tubes filled at intervals with small charges of flash powder. They could be held in the hand and fired, *piff, piff, piff,* one charge after the other, quite harmlessly. Small holes were bored in the profiled ships where the guns ought to be and the squibs were forced into place, dozens of them for the entire fleet. Tommy Thompson, our head electrician, wires these squibs so they could be fired on cue from a small dry battery.

And so off we went in Dutch Schultz's big Pope Toledo, heading for the beach at Santa Monica, where there were never any crowds and we could work without disturbance. Ed Buskirk came along and so did Tommy Thompson, ostensibly to be of service but actually because a ride to the beach was a rare treat and they weren't passing up any rare treats. Cash Shockey cut himself in on the deal for the same reason. And at the last moment Props, our studio dog, came running out to leap into the car and settle himself down for a nice long ride. . . .

We parked at the beach near the Santa Monica pier and set up the profile, adjusted the squibs and the wiring, and then we had nothing to do but wait for the sun to go down and the light to become just gray enough to match the gray of the profile. The profile was adjusted until the bottom edge was in exact line with the horizon. The gray looked awfully dark against that brilliant sky and sea. But the sky would pass through gradations of gray as the day waned, until it would become absolutely black. The trick was to catch it at the exact moment when the gray of the distance matched the gray of the profile.

I kept watching, watching, watching through the camera as the two colors came closer and closer together. One thing was absolutely certain: there would be no doubt about this being sea because it *was* sea, with an incoming tide and three-foot-high breakers, with rows of pelicans gliding and diving in the water just a little way offshore.

The magic moment came. I closed the camera, slipped the pressure pad into place, double-checked everything, and began to turn. After twenty feet had gone through, I gave the go-ahead to Tommy Thompson, who touched wires together. There was one horrible moment when nothing happened. If anything had gone wrong with the wiring, there'd be no time to find it, because the moment of color matching

could not last for long and it would be twenty-four hours before the light conditions would occur again.

But then the guns began to fire, and fire, and kept on firing. I didn't know how long it took a crew to fire and reload a sixteen-inch gun, but these crews of the future were managing it in something between two and two-and-one-half seconds. But maybe in fifty years or so big guns could be fired that fast, who could tell? Almost anything could be happening by 1964.

By the time those squibs had burned out, the light was gone, so swiftly does the light change at sunset. But we had plenty of film in the box before the light change destroyed the illusion, so we packed up and headed for home.

Thus far I had not spent any of Frank Woods's dollar, so I splurged by offering to stand treat for beers all around. The offer was gratefully accepted, and Dutch pulled up at the first saloon we came to. I couldn't go with them because it would be four years and three months before I would be allowed to enter a saloon. But Tommy Thompson took the dollar, and I waited outside with Props until they came out again. Tommy was an honest man. He gave me the sixty-cents change and away we went, not to stop until we drew up at the studio gate.

The shot was wonderful on the screen. Everything worked exactly right. That was a real fleet on a real sea, and if you don't believe it, just look at those pelicans, swooping and diving and sailing in formation over those tumbling breakers. Griffith smiled and murmured, "That is very fine." Which was reward enough for anyone. Praise from Caesar.

KARL BROWN
Adventures with D. W. Griffith, 1973

Irving Thalberg, the frail and youthful producer who is credited with being the creative force behind Metro-Goldwyn-Mayer's enormous success in the 1920's and 1930's, inspired a host of tales during his sixteen years in Hollywood. The most persistent concerned the interminable delays endured by actors, writers, and directors before they met with Thalberg to discuss current or future projects. It fell to humorist S. J. Perelman to explore the comic aspects of their predicament in a short story, "And Did You Once See Irving Plain?"

From the air of immediacy surrounding our project, we figured it would be all of noontime before Thalberg summoned us to impart his hopes and dreams for the script. When three days elapsed with no manifestation, however, I grew restive and phoned. His secretary reassured me at length. Our picture was high on the agenda, but Mr. T. had two in production and was working around the clock; she would advise us the instant he was free. Since it was fatuous to proceed without some clue to what he wanted, we settled down resignedly to wait. Inside of a week, the tedium was well-nigh claustrophobic. Even by reading the trade papers, Louella Parsons' column, and Dostoevsky's prison memoirs, we barely got through the mornings, and the antlike industry of our colleagues discouraged fraternization. Possibly the most consecrated was a writer just across the hall, whose creative habits seemed to derive from science fiction. He customarily wore on his head, while dictating into the mouthpiece of an Ediphone, a scalp vibrator resembling a metal cocktail shaker, which oscillated so busily that you wondered what his dialogue would sound like when transcribed. I subsequently saw the movie he worked on and can testify that I left the theater deeply shaken.

Languishing through our fourth week, I again rang up Thalberg's office and again was counseled patience; the audience was just around the corner. Our agent, Kolodny, who checked us at intervals like a lobsterman visiting his pots, scolded me roundly for fidgeting. He besought us to lie doggo, collect the weekly stipend, and thank our lucky stars that we were eating. That night, on our way home from the jute mill, my wife stopped off in Westwood and bought an ambitious needlepoint design and a dozen hanks of yarn. I ransacked the stores for a narwhal tusk or a bit of whalebone wherewith to execute some scrimshaw work, but none being available, compromised on a set of Boswell and a handbook of chess problems. . . .

As another ten days dragged by, my wife and I seriously began to question whether Thalberg even existed, whether he might not be a solar myth or a deity concocted by the front office to garner prestige. . . .

. . . three weeks later my wife and I decided we had reached the breaking point, and spitting on each other's hands, began work on the screenplay of *Greenwich Village*. After all, we reasoned, we could hardly be accused of insubordination when we'd waited so long in vain for orders. We were waist-deep in clichés one morning, portraying Joan Crawford's anguish at the onslaught of a lecherous etcher, when Thalberg's secretary phoned: we were to present ourselves instanter at his bungalow. Thunderstruck and wrangling over how best to comport ourselves, we hastened toward the Palladian stucco edifice that contained his unit. Cooling their heels in the anteroom were a dozen literary artisans of note like Sidney Howard and Robert Sherwood, George S. Kaufman, Marc Connelly, S. N. Behrman and Donald Ogden Stewart. The epigrams inspired by such a galaxy may well be imagined, but by winnowing them, I discovered that everybody there had been seeking Thalberg's ear without success and was seething. In a few moments, the door of his lair opened, someone of the caliber of Pirandello or Molnar emerged, and to our intense surprise, the secretary waved us in. The resulting epigrams may well be imagined. I forget what they were, but they made my cheeks flame at the time.

The room in which we found ourselves was very long, bathed in shadow and reminiscent of an advertisement for Duo-Art Pianos. Picked out in a single beam of light at the far end was a frail gentleman with intense eyes which he kept fixed unwinkingly on us during our

trip to his desk, barely a matter of two minutes. After routine salutations, he inquired if we saw any possibilities in *Greenwich Village*. I replied that they were limitless and that we were already busily at work on the screenplay.

"Oh, you are, are you?" said Thalberg with marked displeasure. "Well, you can stop right now. I don't want a word on paper—I repeat, not a single word—until we've found the answer to the question."

"The question?" I repeated uncertainly.

"That's right," he said. "The all-important question your story raises —namely, should a woman tell?"

There was a short, pregnant silence, approximately long enough to consume a slice of poppyseed strudel, and my wife leaned forward. "Should a woman tell what?" she asked with almost Japanese delicacy.

"Why, the truth about her past," returned Thalberg, like one addressing a child. "In short, should a beautiful, sophisticated woman confess her premarital indiscretions to her fiancé?"

Before the beautiful, sophisticated woman beside me could confess that this was her first inkling of any such problem in the story, she was saved by the Dictograph. Some Olympian personality, whose voice contained enough gravel to pave the Cahuenga Pass, was calling to borrow a cupful of proxies, and halfway through his plea, word arrived from Miss Garbo that Western civilization would collapse unless Thalberg hastened on the double to Stage 9. The next my wife and I knew, we were blinking in the sunlight outside the building, the same suspicion burgeoning in our breasts. Neither of us put it into words, but we were both right. At suppertime that evening, Kolodny phoned to say that we could sleep as late as we wished the following morning. *Greenwich Village* had been shelved and we were back on the auction block.

S. J. PERELMAN
"And Did You Once See Irving Plain?" 1957

Metro-Goldwyn-Mayer's 1926 production of Ben-Hur *is one of several ill-fated multimillion-dollar films that have become a part of Hollywood folklore. After two years of filming in Italy and California, during which both the leading man and the director were replaced, Ben-Hur's climactic chariot race was finally ready to be shot. British producer-director Kevin Brownlow recreates the events of that day and the unpublicized but vital technical work that followed.*

Saturday was a Roman holiday for the film colony. Among the thousands who crammed the Circus Maximus were stars of the magnitude of Douglas Fairbanks and Mary Pickford, Harold Lloyd, Lillian Gish, Colleen Moore, Marion Davies, and John Gilbert. . . . Directors, too, turned up en masse; Reginald Barker, a fine action director himself, George Fitzmaurice and Henry King, both of whom had recently worked in Italy, Sidney Franklin, Rupert Julian, and Clarence Brown.

Since this was to be the most spectacular moment in an epoch-making picture, Fred Niblo arrived to superintend operations from a high platform. B. Reaves Eason and his assistant Silas Clegg, continued directing from ground level.

Forty-two cameramen were hired for the event. Their cameras were concealed in every position that might yield an effective angle. They were hidden behind soldiers' shields, concealed in the huge statutes on the Spina, buried in pits, mounted on overhead parallels . . .

The crowd was split into sections, and each section was under the control of an assistant director. Urgent calls had gone out for extra assistants, and among those who had offered their services was a young man from Universal, William Wyler.

"I was given a toga and a set of signals," recalled Wyler. "The signals were a sort of semaphore, and I got my section of the crowd to stand up and cheer and to sit down again, or whatever was called for. There must have been thirty other assistants doing the same job. People have said that I was the assistant director on the entire sequence, but that's all I had to do."

Thirty-four years later, Wyler was to direct M-G-M's second version of *Ben-Hur*.

There were twelve chariots and forty-eight horses. Stunt men drove ten of them, and Bushman and Novarro rode their own for this special day. The stunt drivers were range riders, polo-pony breakers, and circus men, as well as being movie doubles. To ensure a real, hell-for-leather, no-punches-pulled epic race, a special bonus was offered to the winner. The fact that the race was fixed for Ben-Hur didn't matter; the day was being devoted to establishing shots with massed crowds. Ben-Hur could win another time.

The incentive given the stunt men stimulated the crowd as well. Once the bets were placed, the assistants no longer worried about whipping up general excitement.

This Saturday was more in the spirit of a carnival rodeo than a filming session. The stunt men put on an astonishing display. During the opening race, a horseshoe flew off one of the chariot teams, hurtled past a camera stand and narrowly missed some spectators. Anxious assistants tried to persuade the crowd to sit down, but the excitement was too intense. By the next race, which was enlivened by a spectacular pile-up, the crowds were responding like the audience at the original Circus Maximus, in Antioch.

At the end of the day, Douglas Fairbanks and Harold Lloyd fought a mock duel with spears, and then the crowds of extras trooped out of the arena, as exhausted as the charioteers themselves.

This one big day had been so impressive that many assumed the sequence was finished. But Eason and his crew spent weeks working in an empty arena on the complicated details of the race—close-ups of racing wheels, thundering hoofs, flaring manes, flexing muscles, and lashing whips. Despite precautions, the inevitable mishaps occurred. When a rescue team of four black horses set out to drag a wreck clear of the arena, Eason arranged for other chariots to flash past them, to increase the excitement. Alarmed by these oncoming chariots, the rescue team panicked and crashed into a camera platform. Eason, who was standing underneath, saved himself by diving between the horses.

In the film, Messala's wheel is wrenched from its axle by Ben-Hur's chariot. Messala crashes, and the other chariots, tearing at breakneck speed around the Spina, cannot avoid him. One after the other, they pile into the wreck, beneath which lies the battered Messala. Ben-Hur races on to victory.

"M-G-M convinced everyone that not a horse had been killed," said Francis X. Bushman. "In that big crash, those stunt men drove straight for the wreck. They knew what to do, and although there were some scratches, and a little blood here and there, none of the men were hurt. Everybody saw the men were okay, so M-G-M say, 'Think of it—not a horse touched!' But there were five horses killed outright in that one crash."

The crash had been planned for a certain turn where ten cameras were positioned. The axle had been sawn through with such careful precision that it broke at exactly the right point.

"The last day we raced," said Bushman, "I was anxious to get home for Christmas. The horses were all wet, and we were pretty exhausted. All of a sudden, smoke bombs went off, pistols were fired, and all hell broke loose. It was our farewell. We shook hands all around, and do you know?—there were tears in our eyes...."

The forty-two cameramen had shot fifty-three thousand feet of film on the big day, but editor Lloyd Nosler had to cope with two hundred thousand feet altogether for this one sequence. On the final show print, the chariot race ran to seven hundred and fifty feet.

But those seven hundred and fifty feet are among the most valuable in motion-picture history. For this was the first time that an action director, realizing the potential of the cinema, had possessed courage and skill enough to fulfill it.

KEVIN BROWNLOW
The Parade's Gone By, 1968

Frank Capra's lavish production of Lost Horizon *remains one of the most popular movies produced in the 1930's. But the version seen by the public differed significantly from Capra's original film. As this excerpt from the director's memoirs indicates, the original failed to please a key preview audience and thereby threatened the careers of both its director and Columbia Pictures executive Harry Cohn.*

Just before photography on *Mr. Deeds*, Harry Cohn invited a studio group to go to a Stanford-U.S.C. football game in Palo Alto. Browsing in the Union Station's newsstand for something to read on the train, I saw a book that Alexander Woollcott had praised on the radio, *Lost Horizon*, written by the English writer James Hilton. I read it; not only read it, but dreamed about it all night. . . .

Next morning, during breakfast in the Lark's dining car, I handed Harry Cohn the *Lost Horizon* book, told him it was the darndest tale I had ever read—a fantastic mystery melodrama about Tibet—and to buy it for me quick, please. He listened and said he'd take Stanford and six and a half points. I went on to tell him there was only one actor in the world to play the lead, Ronald Colman, and that the film would probably cost two million dollars. He dropped his fork.

"Two MILLION? For chrissake, that's half our whole year's budget!" No Columbia picture had as yet cost more than one-fourth that amount. But my enthusiasm for the book ran so high Cohn placated by saying he would buy a six months' option on the story and wait until he saw what *Mr. Deeds Goes to Town* would do at the box office. *Mr. Deeds* went to town in a Brinks' money truck, so Cohn crossed all his fingers, kissed the mezuzah, and went for the two million—proving him to be half-mad, but all gambler. Two million dollars!—five times the cost of *Mr. Deeds*—to spend on a far-out fantasy the like of which had no precedent, no trend to back it up? Columbia's New York executives thought Cohn was half-mad and all *nuts*.

But Cohn had a bigger hunch about *Lost Horizon* than I did—though he never read the book. But that's the way films got made in Hollywood: Back the hot crapshooter who had rolled four sevens in a row—let the winnings ride on his fifth roll. My hand shook as I rattled the dice. . . .

The musty studio projection room was packed solid with friends, Cohns, and Landsmen—two-deep in the seats and three-deep along the walls. They had come to bury or to praise Caesar Cohn for having spent two million dollars on one film (equaling the combined cost of Columbia's other twenty pictures made that year). The air was so thick with hopes and doubts you could finger-write your name in its smog.

The lights dimmed. The main title, *Lost Horizon*, flashed on the screen. Everyone took a deep breath. The chips were down in the ever-bitter feud between hunch-playing President Cohn and his more conservative New York partners. If *Lost Horizon* was a bust Cohn the Crude would get the old heave-ho. . . .

The lights came on [after the screening]. The packed audience remained hushed and still for what seemed like an eternity. Finally Dorothy Howell, my first Columbia scenarist, broke the spell: "If that isn't the greatest picture I ever saw, I'll eat the film inch by inch." That triggered the verbal tom-toms. A relieved Cohn barked out a typical Cohn-ism: "I got news for you lousy experts. In three hours I didn't wiggle my ass once." The crowd guffawed. All knew that Cohn judged films by the seat of his pants. His tail was his guru. Whenever it got bored and scrunched around, it told Cohn the picture was a bust.

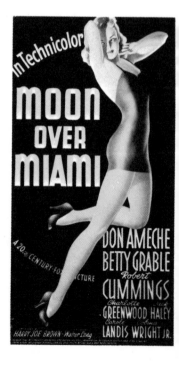

Cohn immediately commanded Columbia's New York executives and board members to fly to Hollywood for a confess-your-sins seminar. I'm sure he told them to bring their noses so he could rub them into their criticisms. The cowed big-wigs would arrive Monday morning. But cagey Cohn—covering against the possibility of *Lost Horizon* being a studio "morning glory" (what the name trainers call a horse that looks like Swaps when racing against stop-watches, but stops and watches when racing against horses)—arranged for a top-secret Sunday night preview at a swank Santa Barbara theater. "If *Lost Horizon* can knock off those Santa Barbara snobs, I got those New York guys right in my pocket."

It was cold and raining hard in Santa Barbara as Lu [Capra's wife Lucille] and I, and Cohn and his new wife, Joan . . . stepped out of Cohn's Rolls Royce to mingle with the big crowd hurrying into the theater. In my excitement I left my hat and overcoat in Cohn's car, but who cared? I welcomed the rain as a good omen. In practically every picture I've ever made there are scenes in the rain—especially love scenes. It's a personal touch. . . .

Opposite the theater the hands of a big four-sided street clock pointed to eight fifty-five. Over the marquee a large banner announced: MAJOR STUDIO PREVIEW TONIGHT! "Damned right it's major," I smirked to myself.

Preview audiences never knew the title of the film, nor the name of the producing company. But experience had taught them to anticipate a film's quality by the heralding symbol that first flashed on the screen: for instance, Leo the Lion's roar, or Paramount's star-circled mountains, usually evoked anticipatory applause—probably because these companies brought their own large claques. When *Lost Horizon* opened with Columbia's Torch Lady trademark, our two wives and Cohn clapped like crazy but their applause was lost in the moans from the audience. The Torch Lady still presaged mediocrity. But we were used to that —and determined, in our time, to change those opening moans into applause.

The Santa Barbara audience sat quietly through the first ten minutes of the film. Then—it began to titter, where no titters were intended. The titters swelled into laughs, where no laughs were intended. I broke out into a cold sweat. The seat of Cohn's pants wiggled so hard his chair creaked out loud. Aghast with confusion, I crawled over people and rushed to the foyer for a drink of water. A well-dressed Santa Barbaran had the same idea.

"After you, sir," I said to him at the drinking fountain. Leaning down for a drink he looked up at me and said: "Did you ever see such a goddam Fu Manchu thing in your life? People who made it should be shot."

I shot out the front door into the rain. The hands of the big clock pointed to nine twelve. Cold with sweat and rain, I walked to Cohn's car for my hat and overcoat. The car was locked. I walked down the deserted street in a daze, my mouth filled with cotton. A lighted drugstore loomed in the rain, I entered, slumped on a fountain stool, ordered a Coke.

It had to be a bad dream. Why should my beautiful poetic saga—which took a whole year to make—exactly the same film that inspired and thrilled us in the studio projection room—be ridiculed in Santa Barbara?

I don't remember how many times I walked around the block, or came back for cokes, or thought of climbing that pitiless street clock to push its mocking hands around to twelve fifteen—but finally, what was left of the audience poured out into the rain and ran for their cars. Their loud, jeering comments about *Lost Horizon* (to paraphrase Ring Lardner) fell like clods on my coffin. The preview was a shambles. *Lost Horizon* was an unshowable, unreleasable motion picture.

For the next two days I walked and walked and walked in a dark trance. Over and over I mentally reconstructed the film—scene by scene, look by look, word by word—seeking the elusive psychological key that made *Lost Horizon* appealing when seen by a few, ridiculous when seen by many.

On the third morning I drove fast to the studio, rushed to the cutting rooms, ordered Gene Havlick, my film editor, to take the main title from the beginning of the *first* reel of the picture and splice it onto the beginning of the *third* reel. No other change. The picture would now be some twenty minutes shorter; its opening sequence: the burning of Baskul. Then I rushed up to see Harry Cohn. He had black pouches under his eyes. I told him about the one change I had made, and that I wanted another preview in a theater—that very night.

"Frank, I can't *hide* another preview from my New York guys. They smell a rat already. Let's show them the picture here in the studio —"

"No, Harry. We *know* a small group will like it. The test is a big crowd in a big theater."

"Goddam you, you know what another disaster like Santa Barbara'll do to Columbia?"

"Yes! It'll wreck Columbia, and it'll wreck you—and *me*."

"What makes you so damn sure throwing away the first two reels will *work*?"

"I'm *not* sure it'll work. But it's the only change I could think of in three days without sleep. Let's preview it again. Invite your New York partners."

Cohn paced behind his desk like a caged tiger. The decision was tough. But he had no alternative. Little flecks of foam whitened the corners of his twisted mouth as he stopped, and said: "You son-of-a-bitch—if this doesn't work—"

There was more than Columbia's hierarchy riding in five limousines to the Wilmington Theater in San Pedro that evening. The mocking Fates were unwelcome hitchhikers.

The same *Lost Horizon*, the same turkey that had laid a catastrophic egg in Santa Barbara, flapped its wings again on the screen in San Pedro—but *without the first two reels*. For Columbia: the moment of truth, as they say in bull rings . . . There was not one laugh or titter in the wrong place! Not in the first ten minutes, not in the whole three hours. The audience was spellbound.

FRANK CAPRA
The Name Above the Title, 1971

In the 1930's Hollywood became a second home for many famous literary figures lured away from writing books or plays by large salaries and the ambience of life in Southern California. Among the most successful was Ben Hecht, who became as well known for the speed with which he could dispatch a screenplay as for the quality of his work.

One of my favorite memories of quickie movie writing is the doing of half the *Gone With the Wind* movie. [David O.] Selznick and Vic Fleming [the director] appeared at my bedside one Sunday morning at dawn. I was employed by Metro at the time, but David had arranged to borrow me for a week.

After three weeks' shooting of *Gone With the Wind*, David had decided his script was no good and that he needed a new story and a new director. The shooting had been stopped and the million-dollar cast was now sitting by collecting its wages in idleness.

The three of us arrived at the Selznick studio a little after sunrise. We had settled on my wages on the way over. I was to receive fifteen thousand dollars for the week's work, and no matter what happened I was not to work longer than a week. I knew in advance that two weeks of such toil as lay ahead might be fatal.

Four Selznick secretaries who had not yet been to sleep that night staggered in with typewriters, paper and a gross of pencils. Twenty-four-hour work shifts were quite common under David's baton. David himself sometimes failed to go to bed for several nights in a row. He preferred to wait till he collapsed on his office couch. Medication was often necessary to revive him.

David was outraged to learn I had not read *Gone With the Wind*, but decided there was no time for me to read the long novel. The Selznick overhead on the idle *Wind* stages was around fifty thousand dollars a day. David announced that he knew the book by heart and that he would brief me on it. For the next hour I listened to David recite its story. I had seldom heard a more involved plot. My verdict was that nobody could make a remotely sensible movie out of it. Fleming, who was reputed to be part Indian, sat brooding at his own council fires. I asked him if he had been able to follow the story David had told. He said no. I suggested then that we make up a new story, to which David replied with violence that every literate human in the United States except me had read Miss Mitchell's book, and we would have to stick to it. I argued that surely in two years of preparation someone must have wangled a workable plot out of Miss Mitchell's Oüida-like flight into the Civil War. David suddenly remembered the first "treatment," discarded three years before. It had been written by Sidney Howard, since dead. After an hour of searching, a lone copy of Howard's work was run down in an old safe. David read it aloud. We listened to a precise and telling narrative of *Gone With the Wind*.

We toasted the dead craftsman and fell to work. Being privy to the book, Selznick and Fleming discussed each of Howard's scenes and informed me of the habits and general psychology of the characters. They also acted out the scenes, David specializing in the parts of Scarlet [sic] and her drunken father and Vic playing Rhett Butler and a curious fellow I could never understand called Ashley. He was always forgiving his beloved Scarlet for betraying him with another of his rivals. David insisted that he was a typical Southern gentleman and refused flatly to drop him out of the movie.

After each scene had been discussed and performed, I sat down at the typewriter and wrote it out. Selznick and Fleming, eager to continue with their acting, kept hurrying me. We worked in this fashion for seven days, putting in eighteen to twenty hours a day. Selznick refused to let us eat lunch, arguing that food would slow us up. He provided bananas and salted peanuts. On the fourth day a blood vessel in Fleming's right eye broke, giving him more of an Indian look than ever. On the fifth day Selznick toppled into a torpor while chewing on a banana. The wear and tear on me was less, for I had been able to lie on the couch and half doze while the two darted about acting. Thus on the seventh day I had completed, unscathed, the first nine reels of the Civil War epic.

BEN HECHT
A Child of the Century, 1954

Although every aspect of the filming of Margaret Mitchell's best-selling novel, Gone with the Wind, *captured public attention, nothing sparked as much interest as the search for an actress to play Scarlett O'Hara. Producer David O. Selznick and director George Cukor spent two frustrating years on their quest before the proper candidate appeared—in a scene as richly dramatic as any in the movie itself.*

The cost of the whole operation [a nationwide talent search] was finally estimated at $92,000, including the tests, of which 149,000 feet were shot in black-and-white and 13,000 feet in Technicolor, a total of more than 24 hours' running time. Later, and privately, both Selznick and Cukor admitted that the results were simply awful. Only during the last few months of the two-year search did columnists and Hollywood colleagues begin to comment rather acidly on the lack of substance behind the glare of spotlights. There were hints that the role was uncastable and the film might never be made. Selznick dealt with this by writing open letters to the columnists, among them the powerful Ed Sullivan, explaining why the film could not be released before 1939 and promising that "the best Scarlett that shows up by the time Gable is available to start work will play the role, willy-nilly."

The most publicized and richly absurd moment of the search occurred on Christmas Day 1937. An outsize package was delivered to Selznick's home by liveried messengers. Ribbons and papers were ripped away to disclose a replica of the novel in its dust jacket, out of which stepped a young girl in crinolines. "Merry Christmas, Mr. Selznick! I am your Scarlett O'Hara!" . . .

Not surprisingly, the possibility that an unknown might be chosen to play Scarlett . . . had its effect on the stars and their fan clubs. As in the case of Gable and Rhett Butler, letters poured in from all over the country—from Europe, too, since the novel was repeating its triumph there—suggesting almost every leading lady of the moment. Many of the ladies suggested themselves. An only halfway satirical article in *Photoplay* noted that "actresses who have never been South of the Slot in San Francisco or below Twenty-third Street in Manhattan, whose closest tie to Dixie in fact, is a faint resemblance to Virginia ham, wander around calling people 'Honey' in a languid, molasses manner." Of the write-ins, Bette Davis was easily the most popular candidate. . . .

By November 1938, ten months after the final meetings with Sidney Howard [author of the original screenplay], there had still been no progress on the script, and there was still no Scarlett; but a date had been fixed for the start of shooting. The deal with MGM specified that Gable had to begin work during the second week of February 1939, and there was no guarantee that he would be available for more than twenty weeks, which was less than the established shooting schedule. . . . Now pressed for time, Selznick announced that a single sequence, the burning of Atlanta, would be shot on December 10, 1938. He planned to use the following two months, until Gable was available, on further preparation and on scenes without Rhett. . . .

The night of the 10th, the night of the fire, was cold. Seven Technicolor cameras—all that were available in Hollywood at that time—had been positioned to cover the burning, of which there could obviously be no retakes, and the set-ups and lighting were worked out by Ray Rennahan, the cameraman-adviser supplied by Technicolor. Pipes had been run through the old sets, carrying gasoline which would ignite them, twenty-five members of the Los Angeles police department, fifty studio firemen and two hundred studio helpers were standing by with equipment and 5,000-gallon water tanks in case the flames should get out of hand. Sets of doubles were engaged for Scarlett and Rhett, who would be seen in various long and medium shots as they escaped from the city with Melanie, her newborn baby, and Prissy the maid hidden in the back of the wagon. A special look-out platform had been built for Selznick, his mother ... and friends. Myron [Selznick's brother] was expected, but had warned he might be late since he was entertaining some clients at dinner.

There was something Napoleonic in the image of the thirty-seven-year-old producer elevated on his platform, surrounded by a court, waiting to give the order that would set the world on fire. However, since Myron was late, the order was delayed—like almost everything else connected with the picture. After an hour, Ray Klune told Selznick that it was impossible to keep the police and fire departments waiting any longer. Intensely nervous ... the producer gave his signal. Instantly the famous old sets, their wood dried for months in the California summer, began to blaze. Cukor called the first "Action!" on *Gone With the Wind*, and the doubles of Scarlett and Rhett made their escape past the burning structures of *King Kong* and *The Garden of Allah*. . . .

As the fire began to wane and the shooting ended, Myron arrived, slightly drunk, with his dinner guests. He led them up to the platform, ignoring David's reproaches and excitedly seizing his arm. "I want you to meet your Scarlett O'Hara!" he said loudly, causing everybody to turn around.

Selznick looked from the acres of burning rubble to a young actress standing beside Laurence Olivier. Firelight seemed to accentuate the hint of pale green in the light blue of her eyes, the green that Margaret Mitchell had ascribed to the eyes of her heroine. He knew that she was Vivien Leigh, an English actress, and that she and Olivier were in love. He also knew that several months ago her name had been mentioned to him by one of his talent executives, and he'd screened two pictures she made in Britain, *Fire Over England* and *A Yank at Oxford*, thought her excellent but in no way a possible Scarlett. Seeing her now, the moment turned into a scene from his own *A Star is Born*. "I took one look and knew that she was right—at least right as far as her appearance went," he said later. "If you have a picture of someone in mind and then suddenly you see that person, no more evidence is necessary. . . . I'll never recover from that first look."

GAVIN LAMBERT
GWTW: The Making of Gone With the Wind, 1973

More than thirty years after her retirement from motion pictures, Greta Garbo retains an uncanny hold on the affection and admiration of the moviegoing public. Clarence Brown, who directed Garbo in several silent and sound movies, recalls some of the qualities that contributed to the Swedish-born actress's profound effect on her audience.

Flesh and the Devil was my first picture for Metro-Goldwyn-Mayer, and it really made Garbo. It also triggered off the Garbo-[John] Gilbert romance.

Greta Garbo had something that nobody ever had on the screen. Nobody. I don't know whether she even knew she had it, but she did. And I can explain it in a few words.

I would take a scene with Garbo—pretty good. I would take it three or four times. It was pretty good, but I was never quite satisfied. When I saw that same scene on the screen, however, it had something that it just didn't have on the set.

Garbo had something behind the eyes that you couldn't see until you photographed it in close-up. You could see thought. If she had to look at one person with jealousy, and another with love, she didn't have to change her expression. You could see it in her eyes as she looked from one to the other. And nobody else has been able to do that on the screen. Garbo did it without the command of the English language.

For me, Garbo starts where they all leave off. She was a shy person; her lack of English gave her a slight inferiority complex. I used to direct her very quietly. I never gave her a direction above a whisper. Nobody on the set ever knew what I said to her; she liked that. She hated to rehearse. She would have preferred to stay away until everyone else was rehearsed, then come in and do the scene. But you can't do that—particularly in talking pictures.

GRETA
GARBO
of
Affairs

from the story by
Michael Arlen—
Continuity by Bess
Meredyth—Directed
by Clarence Brown

with

LEWIS
STONE

JOHN MACK
BROWN

DOUGLAS
FAIRBANKS, JR.

We could never get her to look at the rushes, and I don't think she ever looked at any of her pictures until many years later. When sound arrived, we had a projector on the set. This projector ran backward and forward so that we could match scenes and check continuity.

When you run a talking picture in reverse, the sound is like nothing on earth. That's what Garbo enjoyed. She would sit there shaking with laughter, watching the film running backward and the sound going *yakablom-yakablom*. But as soon as we ran it forward, she wouldn't watch it.

She took her work seriously, though. Her attitude was this; she came on the set at nine, made up and ready for work. She worked hard. At five thirty or six, when she was done, she was through. That was it. There was always a signal on the set—her maid would come in and hand her a glass of water. She would then say good night and go home. And when she was outside the studio, she wanted her life to remain her own. She didn't think her privacy belonged to the public. She used to say: "I give them everything I've got on the screen—why do they try to usurp my privacy?"

Greta Garbo did the greatest thing for a company that any star, living or dead, has ever done. She had a fanatical following in the United States, but unfortunately all those fans were not enough. Her pictures opened to bigger grosses than any other pictures we handled, but they didn't hold the extended run. Once the fanaticism was over, the box-office takings went way down.

On the other hand, in Europe, Garbo was queen. Over there, Garbo was first, second, third, and fourth. In 1942, M-G-M made a picture called *Two-Faced Woman*, but it wasn't rated very highly. Number one, that scared Garbo. Number two, tht war started, the European market was virtually finished, and her American takings fell.

Under the terms of her contract, M-G-M were obliged to pay her whether they made another picture or not—win, lose, or draw. The company couldn't afford to make another Garbo film without the vital European market, and she understood the situation. She went to Mr. Mayer and released him from the contract for two hundred and fifty thousand dollars. She never took a nickel of the rest of the money she was entitled to under the contract. Is there a motion-picture star in the world who would do that? I wouldn't. But that's Garbo. . . .

Flesh and the Devil had a horizontal love scene—one of the first. Toward the end of the scene, Gilbert, playing Garbo's lover, throws a cigarette out of the window. Marc MacDermott, playing Garbo's husband, is getting out of a cab when the cigarette falls at his feet. He looks up at the window, so the audience knows he's prepared for something. When he bursts in on them and finds them in this compromising position on the couch, I put the camera down by MacDermott's hand. I shot through his fingers at Garbo and Gilbert as he clenched his fist over them.

MacDermott challenges Gilbert to a duel. I shot this in silhouette. The two men started back to back, then they walk out of picture. There are two bursts of smoke from each side of screen. We dissolve out to a shot over Garbo's shoulder as she tries on a black hat in a millinery shop. In her hand is a handkerchief with a black border. She has a slight smile on her face. That's how we told who was shot—without a subtitle or any other sort of explanation.

KEVIN BROWNLOW,
The Parade's Gone By, 1968

The credit "Samuel Goldwyn Presents" appeared above the title of many of Hollywood's finest films, including Wuthering Heights, The Little Foxes, *and the 1964 Academy Award winner,* The Best Years of Our Lives. *The playwright Lillian Hellman, who worked on several scripts for Goldwyn, offers an intriguing portrait of this pioneering film-maker in the second volume of her memoirs,* Pentimento.

Soon after *The Children's Hour* I had had an offer to write movies for Samuel Goldwyn. I think Mr. Goldwyn was in his early fifties when we first met, but he was so vigorous and springy that I was not conscious of his age for many years. He was, as were many of the bright, rough, tough lot that first saw the potential of the motion picture camera, a man of great power. Often the power would rise to an inexplicable pitch of panic anger when he was crossed or disappointed, and could then decline within minutes to the whispered, pained moral talk of a loony clergyman whimpering that God had betrayed him. What I liked best were not Mr. Goldwyn's changes of English speech, although some of them were mighty nice and often better than the original. Certainly "I took it all with a dose of salts" is just as good as a grain; the more famous "a verbal contract isn't worth the paper it is written on" makes sense; he meant to be courteous the day he called down "Bon voyage to all of you" to those of us on the dock, as he, a passenger, sailed away; and when, soon after the war, he was asked to make a toast to Field Marshal Montgomery, and rose, lifted his glass, and said, "A long life to Marshall Field Montgomery Ward," one knew exactly why. But I liked best his calculated eccentricities. When he needed a favor or had to make a difficult bargain and knew a first move was not the best position from which to deal, he was brilliant. I was in his office when he wanted an actor under contract to Darryl Zanuck and demanded that Zanuck's secretary call him out of a meeting. After a long wait, Mr. Goldwyn said into the phone, "Yes, Darryl? What can I do for you today?" And a few years after the McCarthy period, during which I was banned in Hollywood, my phone rang in Martha's Vineyard. Mr. Goldwyn's secretary and I had a pleasant reunion, she said he had been trying to reach me for two days to ask if I wanted to write *Porgy and Bess*. After a long wait Mr. Goldwyn's voice said, "Hello, Lillian, hello. Nice of you to call me after all these years. How can I help you?"

But I think our early days together worked well because I was a difficult young woman who didn't care as much about money as the people around me and so, by accident, I took a right step within the first month of working for Mr. Goldwyn. I had been hired to rewrite an old silly, hoping I could make it O.K., to be directed by Sidney Franklin, a famous man who had done many of the Norma Shearer pictures. It was then, and often still is, the custom to talk for weeks and months before the writer is allowed to touch the typewriter. Such conferences were called breaking the back of the story and that is, indeed, an accurate description. We, a nice English playwright called Mordaunt Shairp and I, would arrive at Franklin's house each morning at ten, have a refined health lunch a few hours later, and leave at five. The next day whatever we had decided would sometimes be altered and sometimes be scrapped because Franklin had consulted a friend the night before or discussed our decisions with his bridge partners. After six or seven weeks of this, Franklin said it was rude of me to lie all day on his couch with my back turned to him, napping. I left his house saying I was sorry, it was rude, but I couldn't go on that way. I took the night plane to New York, locked myself in with some books, and the first telephone call I answered two days later was from Mr. Goldwyn, who said if I came back immediately I could go to a room by myself, start writing, and he'd give me a raise. I said I'd think about it, didn't, and left for Paris. When he found me there a week later he offered a long-term contract with fine clauses about doing nothing but stories I liked and doing them where and when I liked. I had become valuable to Mr. Goldwyn because I had left him for reasons he didn't understand. For many years that made me an unattainable woman, as desirable as such women are, in another context, for men who like them that way.

LILLIAN HELLMAN
Pentimento, 1973

Although Citizen Kane *is often thought to be the personal creation of Orson Welles, the film's screenplay was written by Herman J. Mankiewicz, a former newspaper reporter, drama critic, and, with seventy-four films to his credit, one of Hollywood's leading writers. Unfortunately, Mankiewicz sometimes let outside interests interfere with his work and elaborate precautions were therefore necessary to assure completion of the script, as collaborator John Houseman recalls.*

In late February, 1940, when I returned with Orson to California, Herman Mankiewicz was flat on his back in a cast with a triple fracture of his left leg. . . . I sat by his bedside and listened while, between grunts, feverish stirrings and panic calls for Sarah [Mankiewicz's wife], he outlined his notion for a film. It was something he had been thinking about for years: the idea of telling a man's private life (preferably one that suggested a recognizable American figure), immediately following his death, through the intimate and often incompatible testimony of those who had known him at different times and in different circumstances.

In one of its earlier versions, the subject of this prismatic revelation had been a celebrated criminal like John Dillinger. . . . Then, while talking with Orson one day, an infinitely better idea had come to him. As a former newspaperman and an avid reader of contemporary history, he had long been fascinated by the American phenomenon of William Randolph Hearst. Unlike my friends of the Left to whom Hearst was now the archenemy, fascist isolationist and labor baiter, Mankiewicz remembered the years when Hearst had announced himself as the working man's friend and a political progressive. He had also observed him as a member of the film colony—grandiose, aging and vulnerable in the immensity of his reconstructed palace at San Simeon. By applying his "prism" notion to a figure of such complexity and stature and adding to it the charisma inherent in the public and private personality of Orson Welles, the possibility of a rich and unusual movie became apparent.

Welles, in his desperate search for a film subject, had snapped at it instantly. So did I when I heard it. After Mank and I had talked for several hours and Sarah had sent dinner up to the room, I phoned Orson from his bedside and told him I was ready to try. He arrived with a magnum of champagne, and we talked on until Sarah threw us out. The next day . . . I made a deal with Mercury Productions for a period of twelve weeks. At Mank's insistence and remembering how badly I myself had worked with Orson peering over my shoulder, it was clearly stated in the agreement that we would do our work without interference. Welles would be shown what there was of the script after six weeks; the rest of it, if he decided he wanted to continue, when we were finished. It was felt by everyone, especially Sarah, that our only hope of getting such a difficult script done in such a limited time was to move Mankiewicz out of his natural habitat—away from distractions and temptations of all sorts. The retreat chosen for us was a guest ranch in the Mesa country near Victorville at the top of the Cajon Pass.

Two days later, we set out for the San Bernardino Mountains in a small caravan that consisted of a studio limousine containing Mankiewicz, prone and protesting in the back seat, with a trained nurse and two pairs of crutches in the front, and a convertible driven by myself, containing a secretary, a typewriter and three cases of stationery and research material. That night the limousine departed and the next day we went to work. . . .

Our days and nights on the Campbell Ranch followed a reassuring routine. Mankiewicz wrote and read half the night and slept in the morning. I got up early, had my breakfast in the main house so as not to disturb him, then went riding for an hour. . . . After that, while I waited for him to come to life, I would edit the pages Mank had dictated the night before, which the secretary had typed at dawn. At nine-thirty Mank received his breakfast in bed. An hour later, having made an enormous production of shaving, washing, and dressing himself on one leg, he was ready for work. This consisted of going over yesterday's material, arguing over changes and seeing how the new scenes fitted into the structure of the whole . . . .

The wranglers' daughters who served us our meals were frightened by our shouting, but we enjoyed our collaboration. Once Mank had come to trust me, my editing, for all our disagreements, gave him more creative freedom than his own neurotic self-censorship. We argued without competitiveness or embarrassment till the middle of the afternoon. At that time Mank, who suffered great pain from the knitting bones in his leg, would retire for his siesta while the secretary and I went over her notes on the day's talk. At six Mankiewicz rose, ready and eager for the great adventure of the day, when I would drive him and his crutches to a railroad bar known as The Green Spot, where we slowly drank one scotch apiece and watched the locals playing the pinball machines and dancing to the Western music of a jukebox. Once a week we visited the only movie, then returned to The Green Spot for dinner. Other evenings we worked until around ten, when I became sleepy from the mountain air. From my bed, through the closed door, I could hear Mank's voice as he continued his dictation, interrupted by games of cribbage which he had taught our devoted secretary.

We were not entirely incommunicado. Sarah drove up every other week to satisfy herself that all was well, and seemed astounded to discover that·it was. Orson telephoned at odd hours to inquire after our progress. On the appointed day, at the end of six weeks, he arrived in a limousine . . . , read a hundred pages of script, listened to our outline of the rest, dined with us at The Green Spot, thanked us and returned to Los Angeles. The next day he informed the studio that he would start shooting early in July on [the Kane] film which, at the time, was entitled *American. . . .*

Finally, after ten weeks, we were done. Raymond, the butler, had spoken his last snide word, and ROSEBUD had been reduced to ashes in the incinerator at Xanadu. The script was more than four hundred pages long . . . . We spent two more weeks going through the pages with machetes—hacking away, trimming, simplifying, clarifying its main dramatic lines and yelling at each other all the time. . . . Then one evening, from The Green Spot, I called the studio and ordered the limousine for the next day. Mank's leg was almost healed, but he clung to his invalid's privileges. He lay alone, groaning, in the rear seat of the limousine and I followed in the convertible as we made the reverse journey through the Cajon Pass, down the steep curves of the San Bernardino Mountains, between the vineyards and orange groves of Azusa, through the slums of Los Angeles to the RKO studio in Hollywood, where, before returning Mankiewicz to Poor Sarah, we solemnly presented Orson with a screenplay whose blue title page read:

AMERICAN
by
Herman Mankiewicz

JOHN HOUSEMAN
Run-through, 1972

During George Cukor's long and productive career as a director, he has worked with many of the screen's most famous actresses. One of his closest personal and professional associations is with Katharine Hepburn, whose multifaceted talent Cukor charmingly recalls.

Kate and I have been friends and collaborators for forty years, and as she once remarked, there's nothing she could now say to me that would disturb me, and vice versa. It's amusing to go back to that first day when she walked into my office at RKO after [David O.] Selznick and I had signed her for *A Bill of Divorcement*. She struck me as completely in command of herself from the first moment, although *her* version now is that she was absolutely petrified and feeling ill and her eyes were red. I remember showing her the costume sketches for the character, and she didn't like them and said so at once, which was typical. She told me that no well-bred English girl would wear clothes like that and began talking about Chanel. I got my own back by criticizing what she had on—it was expensive but I thought it stank, and I said so—and then taking her to the makeup department to have her hair cut. When we

began shooting the picture, she had this remarkable assurance. . . . During the scene with Jack Barrymore . . . when he comes home and she watches him from the stairs—I discovered later that she thought on the first take he was doing too much. She looked at this famous actor with "the cold eye of youth," as she called it, and made her own evaluation. Imagine, it was the first scene she had to play with him, on her first picture, and she was able to think this, and hide what she was thinking, and act away during the take! Another time, during the shooting, she said to me, "Just because you don't know what you're doing, don't take it out on us!" You've got to be naturally tough with yourself to be so tough with other people. When she met Tallulah, "your friend Miss Bankhead," as she called her, she criticized her to me for using too much bad language. . . . Once, during *Little Women*, I actually hit Kate. (Not hard enough, probably.) She had to run up a flight of steps carrying some ice cream, and I told her to be very careful because we didn't have a spare of the dress she was wearing, so she *mustn't* spill that ice cream. But she did and ruined the dress, and then she laughed—and I hit her and called her an amateur. But, of course, she was immensely professional. During *Little Women* some of the sound men were on strike, and we had a makeshift, inexperienced crew, and Kate had to do take after take of a very emotional scene simply because the sound men kept messing it up. After the fifteenth take, or whatever, they got it—and Kate was so exhausted and agonized by all that weeping, she threw up. But not *until* we'd got the take. There's a lot of Kate herself in some of the pictures we did together, and you'll find different views of her character in the impatient anti-establishment young girl of *A Bill of Divorcement*, the New England side in *Little Women*, independent and idealistic, and in *The Philadelphia Story* the self-willed, apparently high and mighty heroine who's a great romantic at heart. Later, when I worked with her and Spencer Tracy together, it was a fascinating combination of opposites. Kate says I was always giving *her* hundreds of suggestions but none to Spence. Well, Spence was the kind of actor about whom you thought, "I've got a lot of things I could say to you, but I don't say them because you *know*," and next day everything I'd thought of telling him would be there in the rushes. Also, I was never sure whether Spence was really listening when I talked to him. He was one of those naturally original actors who did it but never let you see him doing it. Kate is one of those originals with a lot of ideas she likes to tell you about. So on *Adam's Rib* and *Pat and Mike* Spence never joined the script conferences, whereas Kate and I worked with Ruth [Gordon] and Garson Kanin and alone by ourselves all the way through. . . . But in one way Spence and Kate weren't opposites at all. The very best actors never talk very much about acting itself—and above all they never talk about it until they've done it. Real talent is a mystery, and people who've got it know it.

GAVIN LAMBERT
On Cukor, 1971

A Chronology of Cinema

American photographer Eadweard Muybridge and engineer John D. Isaacs develop process for taking motion pictures — 1872

1874 — First major exhibit of Impressionist paintings held in Paris

Edison Company begins manufacturing peep shows — 1893 — Tchaikovsky dies a few days after conducting premiere performance of his Sixth Symphony

First Kinetoscope parlor opens in New York City under license from the Edison Company — 1894 — Karl Marx completes second volume of *Das Kapita*

Louis and Auguste Lumière devise single machine for photographing and showing movies; first public exhibition of the Lumière process in Paris — 1895 — Wilhelm K. Röntgen publishes results of experiments with x-rays; end of Sino-Japanese War

First public showing of Vitascope film projection system invented by Thomas Armat; Lumière's Cinématographe begins operation in New York City; William Dickson introduces another projection process, American Biograph — 1896 — Production of Anton Chekhov's *The Seagull*

1898 — Blowing up of U.S.S. *Maine* leads to Spanish-American War

George Méliès's *A Trip to the Moon*, based on stories by Jules Verne and H. G. Wells, makes use of special effects and trick photography — 1902

Edwin S. Porter's *The Great Train Robbery* shows flexibility of new medium through use of cross-cuts and close-ups — 1903 — Orville and Wilbur Wright design first airplane

Charles Pathé produces "films d'art" featuring famous stage performers in classic theater roles; release of William Selig's *The Count of Monte Cristo*, first film produced in California — 1908

Thomas Edison organizes major film companies into the Motion Picture Patents Company to cut competition; organization later ruled illegal — 1909 — Expedition led by Robert E. Peary reaches the North Pole

Mack Sennett's Keystone Company produces first of many silent film comedies featuring Ben Turpin, Fatty Arbuckle, Mabel Normand, and Charles Chaplin — 1912 — Chinese Republic proclaimed; Marcel Proust completes his multivolume novel, *Remembrance of Things Past*

1913 — Premiere performance of Igor Stravinsky's *Le Sacre du Printemps*

1914 — Assassination of Archduke Francis Ferdinand of Austria in Sarajevo sparks World War I

Release of *The Birth of a Nation*, D. W. Griffith's masterful story of the Civil War and Reconstruction; a year later Griffith produces *Intolerance*, his most complex and costly film — 1915

1917 — Bolshevik Revolution overthrows Romanov regime in Russia

Douglas Fairbanks, Sr., Mary Pickford, D. W. Griffith, and Charles Chaplin form United Artists, a distributing company for their films — 1919 — Treaty of Versailles signed, ending World War I; Walter Gropius founds the Bauhaus in Germany

Will Hays appointed president of the Motion Picture Producers and Distributors of America, the film industry's self-censoring organization; Robert J. Flaherty's saga of Eskimo life, *Nanook of the North*, shows potential of documentary films — 1922 — James Joyce's *Ulysses* published in France

American inventor Lee de Forest produces one-reel and two-reel shorts with sound recorded on film — 1923 — First performance of Bernard Shaw's *Saint Joan*; Adolf Hitler writes *Mein Kampf*

Metro-Goldwyn-Mayer, largest Hollywood studio, formed through merger; Erich von Stroheim directs *Greed*, shot entirely on location in San Francisco — 1924 — George Gershwin composes *Rhapsody in Blue*

Charles Chaplin produces his classic silent screen comedy, *The Gold Rush*; Sergei Eisenstein directs *Potemkin* — 1925

Abel Gance's *Napoléon* introduces triple-screen projection — 1926 — Publication of Ernest Hemingway's novel *The Sun Also Rises*

Al Jolson stars in *The Jazz Singer*, first feature — 1927

	Year	
film to use recorded music and dialogue; Warner Brothers' *Lights of New York*, earliest all-talking film, opens a year later		
Academy Awards for motion picture excellence presented for the first time; Walt Disney produces *Steamboat Willie* with Mickey Mouse	1928	Bertolt Brecht and Kurt Weill collaborate on the ballad opera *The Threepenny Opera*
	1929	Stock market crash on Wall Street leads to world-wide economic depression
Peter Lorre stars in Fritz Lang's psychological thriller *M*; D. W. Griffith directs his last film	1931	Japanese invasion of Manchuria
Technicolor Corporation discovers a three-color film process	1932	
The Marx Brothers' *Duck Soup* is one of the highlights of a period known for zany comedies	1933	
British director Alfred Hitchcock's *The Thirty-Nine Steps* demonstrates his mastery of suspense genre; Fred Astaire and Ginger Rogers star in *Top Hat*, the archetypal Hollywood musical	1935	Culmination of the legendary "long march" of the Red Army in China led by Mao Tse-tung
La Cinémathèque Française, national archive of film, is founded in Paris.	1936	
Jean Renoir directs *Grand Illusion*, a drama set during World War I	1937	
Release of John Ford's classic Western, *Stagecoach*; David O. Selznick's film version of *Gone with the Wind* becomes one of the most commercially successful films in motion picture history	1939	German invasion of Poland begins World War II; forces under General Francisco Franco are victorious in Spanish Civil War
Orson Welles directs and stars in the controversial *Citizen Kane*	1941	Japanese attack on Pearl Harbor brings the United States into World War II
Sergei Eisenstein publishes *The Film Sense*	1943	
Roberto Rossellini's *Open City* ushers in period of Italian neorealism	1944	Allied invasion of Normandy
	1945	Atomic bomb dropped on Hiroshima and Nagasaki; Germans and Japanese surrender, ending World War II; United Nations charter signed by fifty nations
First Cannes Film Festival	1946	
Ten writers, producers, and directors are jailed for refusing to testify before House Committee on Un-American Activities investigating alleged Communist subversion of the motion picture industry; other artists blacklisted for not cooperating; investigation continues until 1952	1947	India gains independence; a year later Mahatma Gandhi is assassinated
American courts order studios to sell holdings in movie theaters	1950	Outbreak of the Korean War
Debut of Cinerama, a three-camera projection technique that brings action closer to viewers	1952	
Twentieth Century Fox's *The Robe* introduces CinemaScope, a wide-screen projection process; 3-D is used in commercial films	1953	Samuel Beckett's tragicomedy *Waiting for Godot* performed in Paris
Jean Luc Godard's *Breathless* launches the "new wave" in French film industry	1959	Fidel Castro gains power in Cuba; opening of The Solomon R. Guggenheim Museum
Federico Fellini's *La Dolce Vita* and Michelangelo Antonioni's *L'Avventura* are masterworks of the post-neorealistic Italian cinema	1960	
François Truffaut directs *Jules and Jim*	1961	Yuri Gagarin becomes first man to orbit the earth; building of the Berlin Wall
Tremendous success of *The Sound of Music* signals revival of movie musicals	1965	Grotowsky founds Laboratory Theater in Poland
Andy Warhol's *The Chelsea Girls* is the first underground film to achieve commercial success	1966	
	1967	Arab-Israeli Six-Day War; first surgical transplant of a human heart performed
Motion Picture Association of America institutes film rating system; Stanley Kubrick produces and directs *2001, A Space Odyssey*	1968	
	1969	American astronauts walk on the moon
U.S. Supreme Court decision on pornography supports increased movie censorship	1973	Agreement signed to end the Vietnam War; renewed fighting in the Middle East
William Friedkin's production of *The Exorcist* threatens to surpass *The Godfather* and *The Sound of Music* in popularity and gross sales	1974	

181

Academy Award Winners

Year	Best Picture	Best Actor	Best Actress	Supporting Actor	Supporting Actress	Best Director
1973	The Sting	Jack Lemmon *Save the Tiger*	Glenda Jackson *A Touch of Class*	John Houseman *The Paper Chase*	Tatum O'Neal *Paper Moon*	George Roy Hill *The Sting*
1972	The Godfather	Marlon Brando *The Godfather*	Liza Minnelli *Cabaret*	Joel Grey *Cabaret*	Eileen Heckart *Butterflies Are Free*	Bob Fosse *Cabaret*
1971	The French Connection	Gene Hackman *The French Connection*	Jane Fonda *Klute*	Ben Johnson *The Last Picture Show*	Cloris Leachman *The Last Picture Show*	William Friedkin *The French Connection*
1970	Patton	George C. Scott *Patton*	Glenda Jackson *Women in Love*	John Mills *Ryan's Daughter*	Helen Hayes *Airport*	Franklin Schaffner *Patton*
1969	Midnight Cowboy	John Wayne *True Grit*	Maggie Smith *The Prime of Miss Jean Brodie*	Gig Young *They Shoot Horses, Don't They?*	Goldie Hawn *Cactus Flower*	John Schlesinger *Midnight Cowboy*
1968	Oliver!	Cliff Robertson *Charley*	Katharine Hepburn *The Lion in Winter* Barbra Streisand *Funny Girl*	Jack Albertson *The Subject Was Roses*	Ruth Gordon *Rosemary's Baby*	Sir Carol Reed *Oliver!*
1967	In the Heat of the Night	Rod Steiger *In the Heat of the Night*	Katharine Hepburn *Guess Who's Coming to Dinner?*	George Kennedy *Cool Hand Luke*	Estelle Parsons *Bonnie and Clyde*	Mike Nichols *The Graduate*
1966	A Man for All Seasons	Paul Scofield *A Man for All Seasons*	Elizabeth Taylor *Who's Afraid of Virginia Woolf?*	Walter Matthau *The Fortune Cookie*	Sandy Dennis *Who's Afraid of Virginia Woolf?*	Fred Zinnemann *A Man for All Seasons*
1965	The Sound of Music	Lee Marvin *Cat Ballou*	Julie Christie *Darling*	Martin Balsam *A Thousand Clowns*	Shelley Winters *A Patch of Blue*	Robert Wise *The Sound of Music*
1964	My Fair Lady	Rex Harrison *My Fair Lady*	Julie Andrews *Mary Poppins*	Peter Ustinov *Topkapi*	Lila Kedrova *Zorba the Greek*	George Cukor *My Fair Lady*
1963	Tom Jones	Sidney Poitier *Lilies of the Field*	Patricia Neal *Hud*	Melvyn Douglas *Hud*	Margaret Rutherford *The V.I.P.'s*	Tony Richardson *Tom Jones*
1962	Lawrence of Arabia	Gregory Peck *To Kill a Mockingbird*	Anne Bancroft *The Miracle Worker*	Ed Begley *Sweet Bird of Youth*	Patty Duke *The Miracle Worker*	David Lean *Lawrence of Arabia*
1961	West Side Story	Maximilian Schell *Judgment at Nuremberg*	Sophia Loren *Two Women*	George Chakiris *West Side Story*	Rita Moreno *West Side Story*	Jerome Robbins, Robert Wise *West Side Story*
1960	The Apartment	Burt Lancaster *Elmer Gantry*	Elizabeth Taylor *Butterfield 8*	Peter Ustinov *Spartacus*	Shirley Jones *Elmer Gantry*	Billy Wilder *The Apartment*
1959	Ben-Hur	Charlton Heston *Ben-Hur*	Simone Signoret *Room at the Top*	Hugh Griffith *Ben-Hur*	Shelley Winters *The Diary of Anne Frank*	William Wyler *Ben-Hur*
1958	Gigi	David Niven *Separate Tables*	Susan Hayward *I Want to Live*	Burl Ives *The Big Country*	Wendy Hiller *Separate Tables*	Vincente Minnelli *Gigi*
1957	The Bridge on the River Kwai	Alec Guinness *The Bridge on the River Kwai*	Joanne Woodward *The Three Faces of Eve*	Red Buttons *Sayonara*	Miyoshi Umeki *Sayonara*	David Lean *The Bridge on the River Kwai*
1956	Around the World in Eighty Days	Yul Brynner *The King and I*	Ingrid Bergman *Anastasia*	Anthony Quinn *Lust for Life*	Dorothy Malone *Written on the Wind*	George Stevens *Giant*
1955	Marty	Ernest Borgnine *Marty*	Anna Magnani *The Rose Tattoo*	Jack Lemmon *Mister Roberts*	Jo van Fleet *East of Eden*	Delbert Mann *Marty*
1954	On the Waterfront	Marlon Brando *On the Waterfront*	Grace Kelly *The Country Girl*	Edmond O'Brien *The Barefoot Contessa*	Eva Marie Saint *On the Waterfront*	Elia Kazan *On the Waterfront*
1953	From Here to Eternity	William Holden *Stalag 17*	Audrey Hepburn *Roman Holiday*	Frank Sinatra *From Here to Eternity*	Donna Reed *From Here to Eternity*	Fred Zinnemann *From Here to Eternity*
1952	The Greatest Show on Earth	Gary Cooper *High Noon*	Shirley Booth *Come Back, Little Sheba*	Anthony Quinn *Viva Zapata!*	Gloria Grahame *The Bad and the Beautiful*	John Ford *The Quiet Man*
1951	An American in Paris	Humphrey Bogart *The African Queen*	Vivien Leigh *A Streetcar Named Desire*	Karl Malden *A Streetcar Named Desire*	Kim Hunter *A Streetcar Named Desire*	George Stevens *A Place in the Sun*

Year	Best Picture	Best Actor	Best Actress	Supporting Actor*	Supporting Actress*	Best Director
50	*All about Eve*	Jose Ferrer *Cyrano de Bergerac*	Judy Holliday *Born Yesterday*	George Sanders *All about Eve*	Josephine Hull *Harvey*	Joseph L. Mankiewicz *All about Eve*
49	*All the King's Men*	Broderick Crawford *All the King's Men*	Olivia de Havilland *The Heiress*	Dean Jagger *Twelve O'Clock High*	Mercedes McCambridge *All the King's Men*	Joseph L. Mankiewicz *A Letter to Three Wives*
48	*Hamlet*	Laurence Olivier *Hamlet*	Jane Wyman *Johnny Belinda*	Walter Huston *Treasure of the Sierra Madre*	Claire Trevor *Key Largo*	John Huston *Treasure of the Sierra Madre*
47	*Gentleman's Agreement*	Ronald Colman *A Double Life*	Loretta Young *The Farmer's Daughter*	Edmund Gwenn *Miracle on 34th Street*	Celeste Holm *Gentleman's Agreement*	Elia Kazan *Gentleman's Agreement*
46	*The Best Years of Our Lives*	Fredric March *The Best Years of Our Lives*	Olivia de Havilland *To Each His Own*	Harold Russell *The Best Years of Our Lives*	Anne Baxter *The Razor's Edge*	William Wyler *The Best Years of Our Lives*
45	*The Lost Weekend*	Ray Milland *The Lost Weekend*	Joan Crawford *Mildred Pierce*	James Dunn *A Tree Grows in Brooklyn*	Anne Revere *National Velvet*	Billy Wilder *The Lost Weekend*
44	*Going My Way*	Bing Crosby *Going My Way*	Ingrid Bergman *Gaslight*	Barry Fitzgerald *Going My Way*	Ethel Barrymore *None But the Lonely Heart*	Leo McCarey *Going My Way*
43	*Casablanca*	Paul Lukas *Watch on the Rhine*	Jennifer Jones *The Song of Bernadette*	Charles Coburn *The More the Merrier*	Katina Paxinou *For Whom the Bell Tolls*	Michael Curtiz *Casablanca*
42	*Mrs. Miniver*	James Cagney *Yankee Doodle Dandy*	Greer Garson *Mrs. Miniver*	Van Heflin *Johnny Eager*	Teresa Wright *Mrs. Miniver*	William Wyler *Mrs. Miniver*
41	*How Green Was My Valley*	Gary Cooper *Sergeant York*	Joan Fontaine *Suspicion*	Donald Crisp *How Green Was My Valley*	Mary Astor *The Great Lie*	John Ford *How Green Was My Valley*
40	*Rebecca*	James Stewart *The Philadelphia Story*	Ginger Rogers *Kitty Foyle*	Walter Brennan *The Westerner*	Jane Darwell *The Grapes of Wrath*	John Ford *The Grapes of Wrath*
39	*Gone with the Wind*	Robert Donat *Goodbye, Mr. Chips*	Vivien Leigh *Gone with the Wind*	Thomas Mitchell *Stagecoach*	Hattie McDaniel *Gone with the Wind*	Victor Fleming *Gone with the Wind*
38	*You Can't Take It with You*	Spencer Tracy *Boys Town*	Bette Davis *Jezebel*	Walter Brennan *Kentucky*	Fay Bainter *Jezebel*	Frank Capra *You Can't Take It with You*
37	*The Life of Emile Zola*	Spencer Tracy *Captains Courageous*	Luise Rainer *The Good Earth*	Joseph Schildkraut *The Life of Emile Zola*	Alice Brady *In Old Chicago*	Leo McCarey *The Awful Truth*
36	*The Great Ziegfeld*	Paul Muni *The Story of Louis Pasteur*	Luise Rainer *The Great Ziegfeld*	Walter Brennan *Come and Get It*	Gale Sondergaard *Anthony Adverse*	Frank Capra *Mr. Deeds Goes to Town*
35	*Mutiny on the Bounty*	Victor McLaglen *The Informer*	Bette Davis *Dangerous*			John Ford *The Informer*
34	*It Happened One Night*	Clark Gable *It Happened One Night*	Claudette Colbert *It Happened One Night*			Frank Capra *It Happened One Night*
32 33	*Cavalcade*	Charles Laughton *The Private Life of Henry VIII*	Katharine Hepburn *Morning Glory*			Frank Lloyd *Cavalcade*
31 32	*Grand Hotel*	Wallace Beery *The Champ* Fredric March *Dr. Jekyll and Mr. Hyde*	Helen Hayes *The Sin of Madelon Claudet*			Frank Borzage *Bad Girl*
30 31	*Cimarron*	Lionel Barrymore *A Free Soul*	Marie Dressler *Min and Bill*			Norman Taurog *Skippy*
29 30	*All Quiet on the Western Front*	George Arliss *Disraeli*	Norma Shearer *The Divorcee*			Lewis Milestone *All Quiet on the Western Front*
28 29	*Broadway Melody*	Warner Baxter *In Old Arizona*	Mary Pickford *Coquette*			Frank Lloyd *The Divine Lady*
27 28	*Wings*	Emil Jannings *The Last Command* *The Way of All Flesh*	Janet Gaynor *Seventh Heaven* *Street Angel* *Sunrise*			Frank Borzage *Seventh Heaven* Lewis Milestone *Two Arabian Knights*

These two award categories were established in 1936, and the first winners were announced that year.

Academy Awards for Best Foreign Language Films

1973 *Day for Night*, François Truffaut (France)
1972 *The Discreet Charm of the Bourgeoisie*, Luis Buñuel (France)
1971 *Garden of the Finzi-Continis*, Vittorio de Sica (Italy)
1970 *Investigation of a Citizen above Suspicion*, Elio Petri (Italy)
1969 *Z*, Costa-Gavras (Algeria)
1968 *War and Peace*, Sergei Bondarchuk (Russia)
1967 *Closely Watched Trains*, Jiri Menzel (Czechoslovakia)
1966 *A Man and a Woman*, Claude Lelouch (France)
1965 *Shop on Main Street*, Jan Kadar (Czechoslovakia)
1964 *Yesterday, Today and Tomorrow*, Vittorio de Sica (Italy)
1963 *8½*, Federico Fellini (Italy)
1962 *Sundays and Cybele*, Serge Bourguignon (France)
1961 *Through a Glass Darkly*, Ingmar Bergman (Sweden)
1960 *The Virgin Spring*, Ingmar Bergman (Sweden)
1959 *Black Orpheus*, Marcel Camus (France)
1958 *Mon Oncle*, Jacques Tati (France)
1957 *Nights of Cabiria*, Federico Fellini (Italy)
1956 *La Strada*, Federico Fellini (Italy)*
1955 *Seven Samurai*, Akira Kurosawa (Japan)
1954 *Gate of Hell*, Teinosuke Kinugasa (Japan)
1953 no award
1952 *Forbidden Games*, René Clement (France)
1951 *Rashomon*, Akira Kurosawa (Japan)
1950 *The Walls of Malapaga*, Alfredo Guarini (France-Italy)
1949 *The Bicycle Thief*, Vittorio de Sica (Italy)
1948 *Monsieur Vincent*, Maurice Cloche (France)
1947 *Shoeshine*, Vittorio de Sica (Italy)

*Academy Award for Best Foreign Language Film first given; awards for special merit had been made in prior years.

Top-Grossing Motion Pictures

The Godfather, Francis Ford Coppola, Paramount Pictures, 1972	$85,000,000
The Sound of Music, Richard Wise, Twentieth Century Fox, 1965	83,000,000
Gone with the Wind, Victor Fleming, Metro-Goldwyn-Mayer, 1939	77,900,000
Love Story, Arthur Hiller, Paramount Pictures, 1970	50,000,000
The Graduate, Mike Nichols, Avco-Embassy Films, 1968	49,978,000
Doctor Zhivago, David Lean, Metro-Goldwyn-Mayer, 1965	47,950,000
Airport, George Seaton, Universal Pictures, 1970	45,300,000
The Ten Commandments, Cecil B. DeMille, Paramount Pictures, 1956	43,000,000
Ben-Hur, William Wyler, Metro-Goldwyn-Mayer, 1959	40,750,000
Mary Poppins, Robert Stevenson, Walt Disney Films, 1964	40,000,000
The Poseidon Adventure, Ronald Neame, Twentieth Century Fox, 1972	40,000,000
*M*A*S*H*, Robert Altman, Twentieth Century Fox, 1970	36,500,000
Fiddler on the Roof, Norman Jewison, United Artists, 1971	35,550,000
My Fair Lady, George Cukor, Warner Brothers, 1964	34,000,000
Butch Cassidy and the Sundance Kid, George Roy Hill, Twentieth Century Fox, 1969	29,300,000
Thunderball, Thomas Young, United Artists, 1965	28,300,000
Patton, Frank Schaffner, Twentieth Century Fox, 1970	28,100,000
The French Connection, William Friedkin, Twentieth Century Fox, 1971	27,500,000
2001: A Space Odyssey, Stanley Kubrick, Metro-Goldwyn-Mayer, 1968	26,895,000
Funny Girl, William Wyler, Columbia Pictures, 1968	26,325,000

Selected Bibliography

Agee, James. *Agee on Film*. 2 vols. New York: McDowell, Obolensky, 1958–60.

Bayer, William. *The Great Movies*. New York: Ridge/Grosset & Dunlap, 1973.

Brownlow, Kevin. *The Parade's Gone By*. New York: Knopf, 1968.

Ceram, C. W. *Archaeology of the Cinema*. New York: Harcourt, Brace & World, 1965.

Chaplin, Charles. *My Autobiography*. New York: Simon & Schuster, 1964.

Croce, Arlene. *The Fred Astaire and Ginger Rogers Book*. New York: E. P. Dutton, 1973.

Crowther, Bosley. *The Great Films: Fifty Golden Years of Motion Pictures*. New York: G. P. Putnam's, 1967.

Geduld, Harry, ed. *Focus on D. W. Griffith*. Englewood Cliffs: Prentice Hall, 1971.

Griffith, Richard and Mayer, Arthur. *The Movies*. New York: Bonanza, 1957.

Jacobs, Lewis. *The Rise of the American Film*. New edition. New York: Teachers College Press, 1968.

Kael, Pauline. *The Citizen Kane Book*. Boston: Little, Brown, 1971.

———. *Going Steady*. Boston: Little, Brown, 1968.

———. *I Lost It at the Movies*. Boston: Little, Brown, 1965.

Knight, Arthur. *The Liveliest Art*. New York: Macmillan, 1957.

Kobal, John. *Gotta Sing, Gotta Dance: A Pictorial History of Film Musicals*. London: Hamlyn, 1971.

Manchel, Frank. *Yesterday's Clowns: The Rise of Film Comedy*. New York: Franklin Watts, 1973.

Pratt, George C. *Spellbound in Darkness: A History of the Silent Film*. Greenwich, Conn.: The New York Graphic Society, 1973.

Ramsaye, Terry. *A Million and One Nights*. New edition. New York: Simon & Schuster, 1964.

Robinson, David. *The History of World Cinema*. New York: Stein & Day, 1973.

Schickel, Richard. *Movies: The History of an Art and an Institution*. New York: Basic Books, 1964.

———. *The Stars*. New York: Dial Press, 1962.

Shipman, David. *The Great Movie Stars: The Golden Years*. New York: Crown, 1970.

———. *The Great Movie Stars: The International Years*. New York: St. Martin's Press, 1973.

Picture Credits

The Editors would like to thank the following individuals and organizations for their invaluable assistance:

John E. Allen, Park Ridge, New Jersey

Russell Ash, London

John Kobal, London

Museum of Modern Art, New York—Mary Corliss

Barbara Nagelsmith, Paris

The following abbreviations are used:

BB   —Brown Brothers

CP   —Culver Pictures

MOMA—Museum of Modern Art

HALFTITLE: Symbol designed by Jay J. Smith Studio FRONTISPIECE: Marcello Mastroianni, Peter Sellers, Clark Gable and Jean Harlow, Elizabeth Taylor and Richard Burton, Alec Guinness, George C. Scott, Greta Garbo, Theda Bara,

Boris Karloff, Harry Langdon, Sidney Poitier, Jeanne Moreau—All MOMA, with exception of Gable and Harlow, Guinness, Garbo, BB; Langdon, CP

CHAPTER 1 **6** New-York Historical Society **8** top, Stanford University Museum of Art; center, MOMA **9** Both: Cinémathèque Française, Paris **10–11** Musée des Arts Decoratifs, Paris (Lauros-Giraudon) **11** MOMA **12** MOMA **13** Both: BB **14** Byron Collection, Museum of the City of New York **15** top, Byron Collection, Museum of the City of New York; right, Cinémathèque Française, Paris (Josse) **16** MOMA **17** MOMA

CHAPTER 2 **18** John Kobal Collection, London **20** Both: BB **21** MOMA **22–23** BB **23** BB **24** top, CP **24–25** BB **25** BB **26–27** MOMA **28** Both: BB **29** BB **30** BB **31** MOMA

CHAPTER 3 **32** MOMA **35** MOMA **36** MOMA **37** Both: MOMA **38** John Kobal Collection, London **40** MOMA **41** MOMA **42–43** All: MOMA

CHAPTER 4 **44** James Abbe Collection **46** John E. Allen Collection **47** BB **48** top, MOMA **48–49** MOMA **49** BB **50** MOMA **51** MOMA **52** MOMA **53** Both: MOMA **54–55** All: MOMA **56** John E. Allen Collection **57** Both: James Abbe Collection **58** All: John E. Allen Collection **59** left, John E. Allen Collection; right, MOMA **60** MOMA **61** Both: MOMA **62** John E. Allen Collection **63** Both: MOMA

CHAPTER 5 **64** John Kobal Collection, London **66** top, MOMA; bottom, John E. Allen Collection **67** MOMA **68** BB **69** CP **70** MOMA **71** BB **72–73** John Kobal Collection, London

CHAPTER 6 **74** John E. Allen Collection **76** John E. Allen Collection **77** Both: MOMA **78** MOMA **79** MOMA **80** John E. Allen Collection **81** BB **82** BB **83** MOMA **84–85** MOMA **85** John E. Allen Collection **86** John Kobal Collection, London **87** MOMA **88** left, MOMA; right, BB **89** BB **90–91** All: Walt Disney Productions **92** BB **92–93** MOMA **93** BB

CHAPTER 7 **94** MOMA **96–97** All: MOMA **98** Both: Cinémathèque Française, Paris (Mondadori) **99** Cabinet des Estampes, Bibliothèque Nationale, Paris (Josse) **100** MOMA **101** MOMA **102** John Kobal Collection, London **103** MOMA **104** MOMA **105** MOMA

CHAPTER 8 **106** John E. Allen Collection **108** MOMA **109** MOMA **111** MOMA **112** MOMA **113** top, BB; bottom, MOMA **115–21** All: MOMA **122** James Stewart in *The Rare Breed*, MOMA; Joan Crawford and Bette Davis in *Whatever Happened to Baby Jane?* MOMA; John Wayne in *Red River*, MOMA; Gloria Swanson and William Holden in *Sunset Boulevard*, BB; Ingrid Bergman, Academy of Motion Pictures; Gregory Peck, Academy of Motion Pictures **123** Spencer Tracy and Katharine Hepburn in *Guess Who's Coming to Dinner?* MOMA; Henry Fonda in *There Was a Crooked Man*, MOMA; Cary Grant in *North by Northwest*, MOMA; Montgomery Clift, Marilyn Monroe, Eli Wallach, Arthur Miller, John Huston, and Clark Gable during filming of *The Misfits*, MOMA

CHAPTER 9 **124** John Kobal Collection, London **126** MOMA **127** MOMA **128** MOMA **129** Both: Cinémathèque Française, Paris **130** MOMA **131** MOMA **132** top left, Les Films du Carrosse; top right, MOMA; bottom, MOMA **133** top left, MOMA; top right, Cahiers du Cinema **134** Both: MOMA **134–135** MOMA **135** bottom, MOMA **135** right, BB **136–39** MOMA

CHAPTER 10 **140** United Artists **142** top, BB; center, MOMA **142–43** MOMA **143** MOMA **144–45** MOMA **145** United Artists **146–47** All: MOMA **148** Production Robert Raymond Hakim **148–49** Columbia Pictures **149** Both: Les Films du Carrosse **150–51** Vanessa Redgrave in *Isadora*, Jane Fonda in *Klute*,

Glenda Jackson and George Segal in *A Touch of Class*, Al Pacino and Gene Hackman in *Scarecrow*, Dustin Hoffman and Jon Voight in *Midnight Cowboy*, Ryan and Tatum O'Neal in *Paper Moon*, Jack Nicholson in *The Last Detail*, Julie Christie in *The Go-Between*, Diane Keaton and Woody Allen in *Play It Again, Sam*, Faye Dunaway and Warren Beatty in *Bonnie and Clyde*, Liza Minnelli in *Cabaret*, Robert Redford and Paul Newman in *The Sting*, Steve McQueen and Ali McGraw in *The Getaway*, Sidney Poitier and Rod Steiger in *In the Heat of the Night*—All MOMA   **152** (Steve Schapiro)

MAKING THE MOVIES   **154–55** John E. Allen Collection   **157–59** John Kobal Collection, London   **160–61** John E. Allen Collection   **162–66** John Kobal Collection, London   **168–69** John E. Allen Collection   **171** John Kobal Collection, London   **172–73** John E. Allen Collection   **174** John Kobal Collection, London   **176–79** John E. Allen Collection

Index